Designing UX: Prototyping

by Ben Coleman and Dan Goodwin

Copyright © 2017 SitePoint Pty. Ltd.

Product Manager: Simon Mackie

Series Editor: Joe Leech

English Editor: Kelly Steele

Technical Editor: Sophie Dennis

Cover Designer: Alex Walker

Dan Goodwin Author Photo: Alistair Power

Published by SitePoint Pty. Ltd.

48 Cambridge Street Collingwood
VIC Australia 3066
Web: www.sitepoint.com
Email: books@sitepoint.com

ISBN 978-0-9943470-8-4 (print)

ISBN 978-0-9953827-1-8 (ebook)
Printed and bound in the United States of America

About Ben Coleman

Ben is co-founder and managing director at fffunction, a design agency in the South West of the UK. He trained as a product designer in the late 1990's and moved into the field of digital design shortly after. In doing so he brought user centred design principles to this relatively new field and has been applying them to digital projects ever since. At fffunction he wears many hats, but can be mostly be found solving design problems, running workshops, organising content into information architectures, sketching interfaces, building prototypes, and testing them with users.

About Dan Goodwin

Dan is the user experience director at fffunction. With a background of twenty years' experience in agency and in-house software and web development, he is an all-rounder with strong technical and people skills in addition to user experience. He loves user research and bringing users and empathy for them into every step of a project.

Dan loves the sea and gets in it or near it whenever he gets the chance. He likes good coffee, good beer, and good and bad flapjacks.

About SitePoint

SitePoint specializes in publishing fun, practical, and easy-to-understand content for web professionals. Visit http://www.sitepoint.com/ to access our blogs, books, newsletters, articles, and community forums. You'll find a stack of information on JavaScript, PHP, Ruby, mobile development, design, and more.

To the loves of my life—Briony & Louie. Plus the awesome fffunction team and our clients who I get to design great products with. — Ben

To fffunction colleagues past and present (they switched me on to the awesomeness of interactive prototypes) and to my family (they didn't do that, they're just awesome). — Dan

Table of Contents

Chapter 2   The Prototyping Process 22

Chapter 7   **Building HTML Prototypes** 146

Chapter 8   Using Prototypes in Your Project

Workflow 177

Foreword

I was lucky enough to attend a workshop run by Dan and Ben—the authors of this book—about prototyping a few years ago. I remember thinking at the time, "I wish there was a book that talked about the what, how, and why of prototyping". So when SitePoint asked me to help co-ordinate a series of books on UX, this particular book was top of the list.

Before reading this book I had no idea you could quickly make a shareable, clickable prototype with nothing more than a Sharpie, some paper, and a clever set of easy-to-use tools; from paper to mobile screen in minutes. There are many ways to prototype and this book helps you take your ideas and make them real.

The power of a prototype is the ability to take user needs, prioritise them and present them back to the project in a way that doesn't require endless documentation. User experience is full of cliches, but it's true a picture *really* is worth a thousand words.

Joe Leech[1], Aspects of UX series editor, Bristol, UK, February 2017

Acknowledgments

Thanks

- Simon, Joe, and Sophie for all their help and guidance
- Laura Nevo for POP and responsive collage work she did with us at fffunction
- Stuart Tayler and Sandra Gonzalez for their prototyping workshops at UXBristol 2016
- James Chudley, Stuart Church, and Dave Ellender for inviting us to run a prototyping workshop at UXBristol 2014 — the origin of this book, as Joe's foreword highlights!

[1.] *http://mrjoe.uk/*

Permissions (and Thanks!)

- Dorothy House (logos, pictures of: workshop affinity post its, style guide, IA, prototype)
- The team at Bristol Museums, Galleries and Archives (logos, pictures of prototype)
- The team at Comma Press and everyone involved in creating MacGuffin (logos, pictures of prototype)
- Fauna & Flora International / Global Trees (for responsive collage)
- Winchester Theatre Arts (logos, pictures of prototypes)
- Chloe Hughes and the team at Theatre Royal Plymouth (pictures of sketching workshop)
- Giles, Richard, James, and the rest of the cxpartners team

Who Should Read This Book

This book is for beginner-level UX professionals, web designers, and developers who want to get a practical introduction to prototyping techniques. No prior experience with prototyping is assumed.

Conventions Used

You'll notice that we've used certain typographic and layout styles throughout this book to signify different types of information. Look out for the following items.

Tips, Notes, and Warnings

 Hey, You!

Tips provide helpful little pointers.

 Ahem, Excuse Me ...

Notes are useful asides that are related—but not critical—to the topic at hand. Think of them as extra tidbits of information.

Make Sure You Always …

… pay attention to these important points.

 Watch Out!

Warnings highlight any gotchas that are likely to trip you up along the way.

Supplementary Materials

- https://www.sitepoint.com/community/ are SitePoint's forums, for help on any tricky web problems.
- **books@sitepoint.com** is our email address, should you need to contact us to report a problem, or for any other reason.

Chapter **1**

Defining the Case for Prototyping

In this chapter, we'll define what we mean by prototyping and what we'll be covering in this book, as well as some of the aspects we *won't* be addressing.

We'll discuss why prototyping is a useful tool in the design process. We'll consider some situations when prototyping is likely to be useful and discuss what prototyping can't do. We'll also address who is likely to benefit from the creation of prototypes and why.

What is prototyping?

Plenty of definitions exist of prototypes and what is meant by the act of **prototyping**. As a result, it's helpful to define what we'll be exploring when we talk about prototypes in this book.

We're talking about creating *something* to test, explore, or communicate design ideas for *a thing* that is being designed.

The *something* is a low-fidelity representation of our *thing*, which might be:

- a simple sketch or series of sketches
- a basic wireframe or wireframes
- wireframes or sketches to which we've added clickable/tappable functionality, allowing users to move between different views and presentations within our *thing*
- a fully interactive implementation, typically with basic design and styling, which implements the functionality and interactivity of the *thing* or parts of it
- a combination of things sitting somewhere in this range of fidelities.

The *thing* is what we're designing. For the purposes of the book, we'll focus on websites—all with varying degrees of interactivity such that some folks might call them 'web apps'. You'll probably find significant crossover with the techniques this book describes being used to prototype the design of native desktop and mobile apps, too.

Beyond the scope of this book, prototypes and prototyping are often used to explore the design of:

- physical products. It's important to prototype these products and user interactions with them. But when we're talking about designing physical things, we move into disciplines (such as 3D design, making, connectivity, and 3D printing) that are beyond the scope of this book.
- processes, systems, or models. When we're talking about these things, we're drifting into service design territory. Again these are things which can and should be prototyped but they're beyond the scope of this book.

It's worth noting that although these kinds of prototypes (and probably others that we haven't described here) aren't explicitly covered by this book, many of the aims of prototyping and a lot of the principles and techniques may still be relevant.

Why use prototypes?

There are some compelling reasons to utilize prototyping, such as:

- testing and communicating user interface designs
- saving time and money
- bringing users into the design process
- engaging stakeholders in a meaningful way
- designing across devices and platforms
- creating and testing with real content and data

Let's explore these in a little more detail.

Testing and Communicating UI Designs

The best way to test our user interface designs is with real users, and the best way to communicate our user interface designs is to implement them. This is where prototypes are significantly more powerful than sketches, wireframes, or flat designs (for example, visual design mockups produced in Photoshop).

Saving Time and Money

As a design progresses through increasing levels of fidelity (such as full production-ready implementation, full content and/or data), the effort (and hence, cost) of implementing that design increases, too. Without getting bogged down in statistics, it's generally accepted that this increase is more exponential than linear, as represented in the figure below.

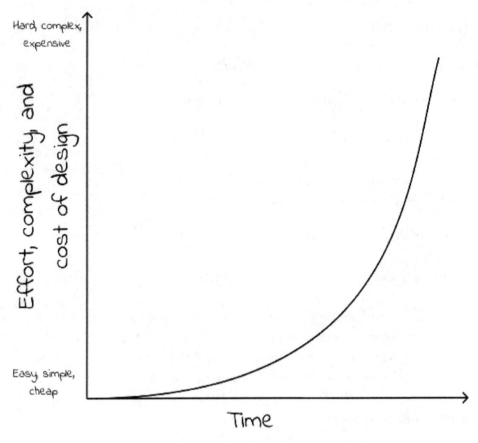

1-1. The cost of implementing design work and changes over time

As a result, placing designs in front of users and stakeholders as early as possible means that we can share, test, discuss, identify issues with, and iterate our designs in an efficient and cost-effective way. Involving the whole project team in the creation of a prototype early in the design life cycle is the recommended way to go about it.

Bringing Users into the Design Process

In situations where we are uncertain about design decisions or are experimenting with ideas--and particularly where we want our designs to work best *for our users*—we should find ways to explore our ideas and test them with users early in the process. Sketches and wireframes provide a great starting point (and, to a degree, sketches and wireframes can be treated as prototypes). We can sketch and wireframe ideas for sections, features, and interactive elements. And if we work collaboratively, we can quickly generate lots of ideas.

Yet putting sketches and wireframes in front of users can only go so far. We can ask users to tell us what they'd do and how they'd approach a specific task, but as interactivity is limited, there isn't much users can actually do. This can be tricky for users in an observed testing scenario (even if it's informal) as people will feel pressured to say *something*, to seem useful. We tend to receive feedback that's subjective, such as "I'd do it this way" or "I'd put a button there"). This is generally unhelpful to us. What we need is to observe users *using* our product, trying out our idea.

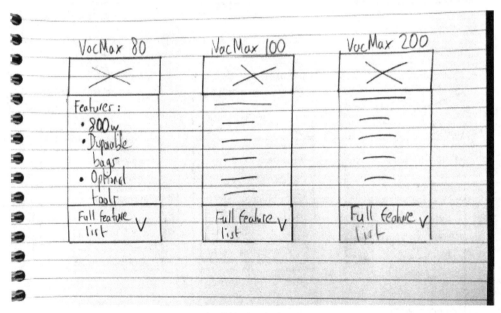

1-2. A quickly sketched prototype

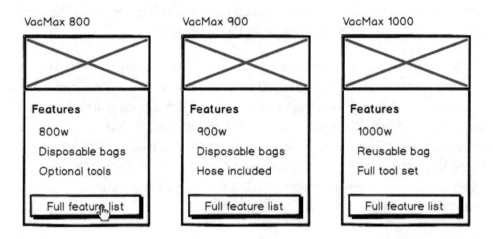

1-3. Creating a quick prototype (here we've used Balsamiq) from our sketch

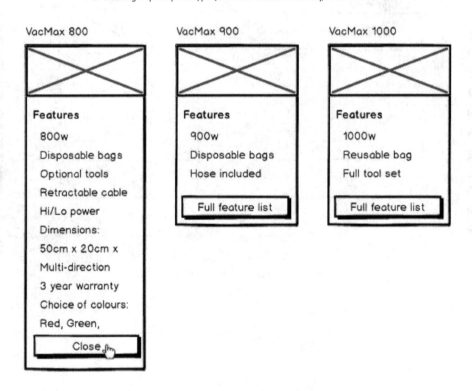

1-4. Balsamiq allows us to add interaction , making for an easier and more powerful user test

This is where prototypes can come in—bridging the gap between ideas, sketches, and wireframes and the later stages where we're producing full fidelity visual designs and production level markup and implementation. They provide enough depth, fidelity, and interaction to make user tests much more relevant. Users can be set tasks that they want to complete (because our user research has told us what are our users' key goals). They are given free rein to explore, interact, review content, see results, and react; to explain where they're going, what they're doing, and why.

Engaging Stakeholders in a Meaningful Way

Regardless of how a project is structured (for example, in-house, client/agency), it will involve multiple stakeholders. Prototypes can help stakeholders understand your designs and involve them in a much more powerful way than abstract deliverables such as user research outputs, sitemaps, sketches, or wireframes.

Stakeholders can interact with a prototype themselves; they can experiment with it, explore, review content and data, and add or change content or data. It's real enough that they can quickly and easily visualize and understand.

Stakeholders are often senior-level people with very little time to spare. A lot of their time is spent being shown boring slide decks full of bullet points and pouring over spreadsheets full of numbers. Getting to play with a prototype is really exciting and different for them, so it's a great way to engage and gain approval quickly.

Additionally, a stakeholder can share a prototype with other people, such as others in the organization who are less involved but interested, third parties whose opinion they value, or users to whom they have easy access.

You might even find stakeholders becoming so involved that they start creating their own sketches and prototypes to communicate their ideas.

Designing across Devices and Platforms

We're now in a world where our designs will be used across multiple devices with different viewport sizes and multiple methods of interaction: touch, keyboard, mouse, remote control. All the indicators are that this device and interaction space will only continue to grow.

Most prototyping tools and techniques support us in designing across different devices, sizes, and forms of interaction to a degree. They achieve this better and more efficiently than sketches, wireframes or flat designs. Some prototyping tools and techniques—in particular HTML prototyping—are particularly helpful here.

Presenting across different devices is a massive leap forward in terms of testing. We can run user tests across several devices, as well as enable users to test prototypes in a familiar context on their own devices. Similarly with stakeholders, we can encourage them to review our prototypes on smartphones, tablets, and other devices.

As we look across the range of prototyping techniques in later chapters, we'll look at comparing their ability—or inability—to help us design and test our prototypes across devices.

1-5. A prototype for a page to help users visit Bristol Museum and Art Gallery on a desktop browser and on a smartphone

Creating and Testing with Real Content and Data

If one of our overall aims is to better involve users in the design of our product or service, as well as to better communicate our designs to stakeholders, the ability to present realistic and convincing *real* content or data makes a significant difference to our ability to meet that aim.

Most prototyping tools and techniques make it easy to incorporate real content into our designs quickly. If we have stored a set of real content with some structure to it, we can generally get an interactive prototype to pull in that content. It could be a database or a set of files that we can query with some code or set as a data source in an interactive prototype. It might even just be content copied and pasted in, but with the benefit of tools to help with layout. Many tools make it easy to build and include a library of images, cropping and resizing as necessary.

Some tools provide separation between content and the presentation of that content. This means that we can start with a prototype with no content or placeholder information, then give our project team and stakeholders (even those with minimal technical knowledge) the ability to add and edit as it becomes available.

1-6. At fffunction, we built a mechanism to load and present real content when we developed a prototype for MacGuffin, a self-publishing platform

We can also allow users to input content to a prototype and for the prototype to work with and respond to that real content. Imagine working on a web app where a user provides some information about themselves and the web app presents a set of results for them to work with. If the user is able to use their own information when testing a prototype and the prototype provides results that reflect the information, the test will be much more realistic and useful. This level of interactivity can only be achieved with a prototype that implements some degree of real data input to present results, offering something a wireframe or sketch never could.

What can we prototype?

In simple terms, what we might consider creating a prototype for are the kinds of things that we might we otherwise use sketches and wireframes to explore and design.

We'll now review some of the items for which prototypes are particularly helpful in the design of a website.

 ### Return of the Native

As we at fffunction have most experience in creating prototypes for websites and web apps, they'll be the sorts of prototypes that we'll focus on in this book; however, a lot of these tools and techniques can be employed to prototype native mobile and desktop applications too. Native applications may bring different requirements such as device dimensions, interaction techniques, and interfacing/ interacting with device hardware (such as camera, audio recording/playback, accelerometers and location). These extra requirements bring greater complexity to the design and arguably make prototyping even more important and relevant.

Information Architecture and Structural Elements

Presenting a site's structure as a sitemap diagram to the project team and stakeholders is often ineffective. It's even harder to user-test structural elements with such a diagram. At a more granular level, we have the same problem testing and presenting other aspects of information architecture including structure, behavior and labelling in navigation, or taxonomies (such as the categories users can employ to segment and query products in an online shop).

It's possible to build an interactive prototype and populate it with real structural elements (for example, primary and secondary page navigation, product categories). Then we can test these structures: the page hierarchy, the behavior of the navigation, and the labels that we're proposing with real users given real tasks to perform. We can present our information architecture to stakeholders in an exciting, tangible way that they can visualize and explore.

1-7. A prototype built to test the structure and navigation of a website for a theater arts school

This lends itself particularly well to the loading of real content for prototyping then being used for production. We can start at a low level of fidelity by loading the structure of a website into a content management system (CMS) database for a prototype. Then we can increase fidelity by adding placeholder content, then further still by adding in real content. This content can then potentially be used in a production implementation. We'll talk about this in detail in Chapter 7.

Layout and Visual Hierarchy

We can use a prototype to design, test, and communicate the overall layout and hierarchy of elements that make up a page. This is the kind of design where we'd traditionally use wireframes.

Take the example of a site presenting a range of vacuum cleaners. We might have a list of all cleaners grouped or categorized in a certain way; for example, a page for each individual cleaner showing specifications, options, and user reviews. We have to decide what content to present in the listing and what to display on a single cleaner page, as well as how to lay them out.

We can use insights from user research to help us, such as the tasks different types of users are trying to achieve, what information is needed to solve those tasks, and what's considered important / less important. From there we can come up with a proposed layout for the listing and for the single page. Then we can implement that proposal in a prototype, ideally using some real content.

1-8. Using an HTML prototype to design layouts for a vacuum cleaner listing page on wide and narrow viewports

A prototype enables us to present the proposal to stakeholders and to test it with real users. Over the lifetime of our prototype, we can add, remove, and change content, as well as alter the layouts we're proposing. We can test small changes or radical alternatives to the layout. If our prototype's implementation has a good separation of content and presentation, the process of changing the layout while maintaining the same base content is easy. That means we can test more layouts, more quickly and more easily.

Interactive Elements

All websites have at least some interactive elements (such as a link), but many have interactive elements that are more involved and complex. This requires significant amounts of user interface design.

Consider the example of an ecommerce site selling clothes and accessories. Users tend to have varying requirements in narrowing their clothing searches, whether it's by size, color, season, garment type, fabric, brand, and so on. This often leads designers of an ecommerce store to consider a **faceted navigation pattern**, where users can narrow their search across several sets of criteria—for example, medium size, yellow color, and cotton fabric—and see the results promptly.

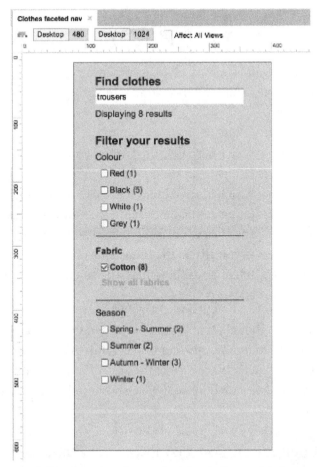

1-9. Using Axure to prototype a faceted navigation user interface

While it sounds straightforward enough, this is a remarkably complicated feature to design. The ability of a prototype to help us try out ideas for laying out categories, their method of interaction, and which categories to narrow results by will significantly improve our chances of doing it justice. We can use a decent set of representative content to quickly implement a range of ideas for presenting and interacting with that content. We can communicate our ideas with stakeholders and test them out with real users—iterating, changing, and experimenting as we go.

Without a prototype, this kind of rapid iteration could only happen once the online store had been (at least) partially implemented. Prototyping allows us to do it earlier, quicker, and cheaper.

What *can't* we do with a prototype?

By now, I'm hoping you have plenty of ideas for a prototype and what can be achieved by creating one. That said, it's worth addressing what we're unlikely to achieve with a prototype.

Use Quantitative Research to Make Decisions

If you're looking to try out some design ideas with a view to employing metrics to assess which is "better" (for example, more sign-ups, more conversions, highest task completion rate), a prototype is unlikely to help. For these kinds of tests, you need a large sample size—typically in the thousands or tens of thousands; however, utilizing quantitative research to make decisions such as these is beyond the scope of this book.

It's worth pointing out, though, that prototypes generally *will* help you test your designs with a large number of users more successfully than alternatives such as sketches or wireframes. This is because of the ease of implementing, sharing, publishing and running tests with prototypes, and iterating these tests over and above the other methods.

Testing for Completion/Conversion Funnel Progress

It's generally a bad idea to try to measure the success of a task completion/conversion funnel (for example, how far users of an ecommerce site progress along a sales funnel) with user tests, whether it be a prototype or with a production site[2].

This is because in an observed user-testing scenario, users are motivated to complete the tasks they're presented with purely by the nature of being a participant in a user test. We might expect to hear comments along the lines of "I'd have given up by now," which to a degree are useful. But since what users say they do and what they actually do can be two completely different things,

---

[2]. Quantitative measurement of progress in goal funnels is covered in the SitePoint book *Researching UX: Analytics*: https://www.sitepoint.com/premium/books/researching-ux-analytics

such comments only help up to a point. When using a site in a natural context, user behavior in reality may be very different and tolerance for poor design much lower.

Testing Accessibility

Most prototyping techniques fail to match the final production implementation and, as a result, can't be used to test the accessibility of a design; for example, measuring the ability for users of assistive technologies to access content and features.

Typically, HTML prototyping is done in a very rough-and-ready way, so coding standards and accessibility barely get a look-in.

An accessible implementation is essential, and best audited and tested on a production site prior to launch and on an ongoing basis. That said, if you wanted to test the accessibility of certain features in a prototype (such as a complicated interactive element), there's no reason why you couldn't build those features to the relevant standards and test them.

Testing the Impact of Visual Design

Generally, prototypes are created at a level of fidelity that is too low to test the impact of visual design features such as font sizes, background colors, or borders on the visual hierarchy of a design.

Some prototyping tools and techniques (such as InVision, discussed in Chapter 6) do allow the creation of a prototype from high-fidelity design mockups. Hence, if you can come up with a sensible user-testing strategy, you could use these to test the impact of your visual design changes.

Being the Sole Source of Documentation

Agile (whether it's little a or big A agile) prefers working software over comprehensive documentation, so it can be natural for some teams to rely solely on their evolving prototype to document what they're doing.

Prototypes on their own don't document the history of creating a design (although a good source-control workflow could help here). Therefore, it's important that you take care to document changes between versions when evolving your prototype. Similarly, a prototype alone won't always show enough to provide sufficient documentation for full design and development. Furthermore, it's too easy for stakeholders or project team members to miss an important feature because they failed to click on that part of the prototype.

To mitigate these problems, consider how you can produce just enough supporting documentation and decision-making history so that the team can understand what's been implemented and why.

Who are prototypes for?

Most likely you're reading this book because you're part of a team working on the design and implementation of a product, and you can see that there might be value in creating a prototype. Here's hoping we're already starting to confirm that there is!

But who else in your project team might benefit from the creation of a prototype over and above your users and stakeholders? If you need to convince them, here are some potential benefits to different project team participants.

Designers

This could include visual designers and/or user experience designers, user researchers, and information architects.

These people will be taking any insights learned from user research and utilizing them to design every aspect of the product including information architecture, user interfaces, visual styles, features, elements, modules, and interactivity.

As already discussed, all of these items can be prototyped, and a prototype is a great way for a team of designers to explore ideas; share and test them amongst themselves and the wider project team and stakeholders; test with users; and iterate.

Developers

One of the problems with static sketches, wireframes, and designs is that it's hard to design and then communicate how a design behaves in addition to how it looks. This is particularly important for developers as they turn designs into functioning production code. To a degree we can annotate static designs to explain behavior, or we can provide supplementary documentation that does the same (such as a functional specification). But it can be hard to describe behavior in this way, and we can expect some back and forth in the team due to misunderstandings and miscommunication. Additionally, annotations and functional descriptions tend to get left behind and forgotten as designs are updated through the lifetime of a project.

Interactive prototypes go a long way to solving these problems. Developers can become involved in creating and using a prototype early on in the design process, along with other members of the team. They can start to understand how a design should behave, and bring their knowledge and judgement of development work when implementing design ideas. And they can start to think about *how* they will implement it, and what kind of data structures and models might be required. Prototypes can help make implementation scoping and estimation more accurate and realistic, which in turn can help the whole project team understand the time and effort involved in implementing a design.

Project and Account Managers

For those running a project and dealing with clients day to day, prototypes help provide extra clarity and fidelity when communicating the project team's design ideas.

Project managers are able to visualize and understand design ideas, and verify they're solving the problems that the design team is tasked with at any given point. With prototypes, they are better placed to talk through and test out design ideas with the project team and stakeholders.

Business Analysts

If what you're working on involves business processes and systems, you may well be working with business analysts. Their job is to understand business problems and processes, and hence contribute to the design of systems that handle them.

If an interactive prototype is built for such a system (or part of it) and then populated with some real data, business analysts are then able to see how the project team's designs work with that data. They can potentially trial the prototype with real end users of the system. If confidence in the prototype allows, analysts may even trial the prototype in a live environment, perhaps alongside an existing system for comparison and potential fallback in the event of problems.

Customer Support Representatives

It's ideal to have people involved with your project who are dealing with users on the front line. They often understand users better than anyone—their problems, goals, and tasks. It's what customer support deal with every day.

If you can put your prototypes in front of customer support staff—either because they'll be using what you're implementing or because they have a good understanding of users who will, you're likely to receive useful feedback and insights. Presenting an interactive prototype that they can explore will make their job of understanding and providing feedback on your design ideas that much easier and productive.

 Prototyping on a Large Scale

> It's worth sounding a note of caution if you're prototyping on large and complex projects with large and changing teams. Avoid allowing a prototype to become the one and only "source of truth" as this can be problematic, as discussed in the section "What *can't* we do with a prototype"

Summary

In this chapter, we've looked at why creating prototypes is a superior way to communicate designs over sketching and wireframes.

We've discussed the benefits they bring in terms of user research and stakeholder engagement, as well as talked about the potential for prototypes to make it easier to design with real content and data across devices.

We've looked at specific circumstances where prototypes should be considered, such as designing complex user interfaces, and where they fall short as an option.

And finally we looked at the different project team roles who are likely to benefit from the creation of prototypes.

In the next chapter, we'll look at the prototyping process and what's required when starting to create a prototype.

Chapter 2

The Prototyping Process

In this chapter we're going to discuss getting started with a prototype. We'll look at the process, including:

- when you should consider creating a prototype
- planning its creation
- gathering resources you might need
- approaches to working on your prototype

Chapter 8 will build on this, going into more depth around how a prototype fits into various project workflows. For now, we'll cover the basics here so that you can start on a prototype today.

When to Prototype

The short and easy answer to this question is: any time, whatever you're working on—now! But there are some specific triggers to watch out for, at which point you're likely to benefit from a prototype, so you should consider building one.

You have an Idea

Maybe you have an idea for a design, or for a feature to add to an existing design; for example, a new approach for browsing products on an ecommerce website. You think it's a good idea but are unsure whether there's a market for the design, or whether users will want to use it, understand it, or value it.

You could ask people if they think your idea is good. If you're adding a feature to an existing site, you could ask the site's users by running a survey. The problem with these approaches is that asking people what they think of an idea, or if they'd use this new feature, tends to be unhelpful. The odds are users will say it's a good idea and that they'd probably use it. And you're not much the wiser.

But if you can present your idea in the form of a prototype and ask people to try it out, the feedback from observing people using your design will be much more helpful.

Buy-in from Others

You may have an idea for a new design and need to build a team around you. You may require investors on board to fund development of an idea. Or you may be in a situation where you have to convince management, stakeholders, or other budget owners in your organization that your idea is worth investing in.

A prototype will help you present your idea in a way that the people you're trying to convince can visualize, experiment with, and get excited about. Investing a little extra time up front will make your pitch that much stronger.

Information Architecture to Visualize, Present, and Test

Information architectures can be unwieldy and hard to visualize and test quickly. Even more so if the structure you're proposing is broad (that is, lots of pages across a few levels), deep (lots of levels going down), or broad *and* deep.

You can build a prototype that presents your information architecture (or part of it) with the structure and/or labelling you're proposing. The prototype will present your structure with an implementation that people can see and explore. This will be much easier to share with your team and stakeholders, and to test with users than any structural diagram.

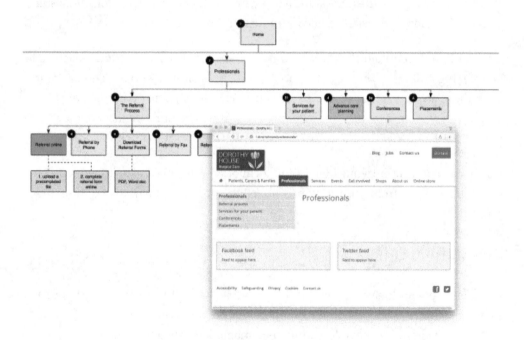

2-1. A prototype can present the structure of a website in a way that's more understandable, engaging, and testable than a structure diagram

A Lengthy User Journey or Several Changes of State over Time

Some designs for a product or feature will have a lengthy user flow, with the user moving across many screens, templates, and elements in order to complete tasks and meet goals. Some will require a user to return to a site or app repeatedly to complete different steps on a user journey. And some will need to present screens and elements in different states at different times throughout a user journey.

In these situations, it can quickly become difficult and unwieldy to develop ideas and explore, communicate, and test your designs when you're limited to producing static sketches, wireframes, and design mockups. An interactive prototype can tie the different screens, elements, and states together, enabling you to communicate and explore these complex interactions and lengthy user journeys. And testing the designs for these journeys with users becomes much more powerful when users can input and see their own information, rather than having to put themselves into test scenarios.

If you find yourself getting bogged down in the complexity of a design, or you think you might, consider prototyping early to save time and effort.

A Pool of Available Users

You may find yourself working in a situation where it's easy and cheap to get to real users who can test designs you're working on.

Examples include:

- an in-house project where you have easy access to staff who will be using your designs
- engaged by a client in a place where you can set up a laptop/tablet and access potential users for quick testing (such as in a museum)
- working on an agile/lean-style project where there are users or user representatives on the project team

In such situations, creating prototypes to place in front of these users can lead to a significant improvement in the quality of your designs, as well as the speed at which you can produce them.

Communicate and Test Designs across Devices

We've discussed in Chapter 1 how important it is to be designing across devices, including presenting and testing your designs across devices.

The power of prototypes to help with this cannot be overstated. It's rare to *not* need a design to work in several devices. So the odds are strong that most people will benefit from a using a prototype here.

Lots of Ideas–or No Ideas–for Solving a Problem

Collaborative working is a terrific way to solve complex design problems. It can result in a multitude of design ideas; indeed, that's a benefit of designing in groups. But how do you decide between ideas?

The process of creating a prototype forces you to think about the practicality and reality of implementing designs. You might start to carry out your idea and then realize that you lack the data required to execute your design, or that although the idea seems good on a paper sketch, in reality it will never work onscreen.

You can also use prototypes to test and compare different ideas. You might start working at a high level with several ideas, weeding out those that perform poorly and implementing others to increasing levels of fidelity.

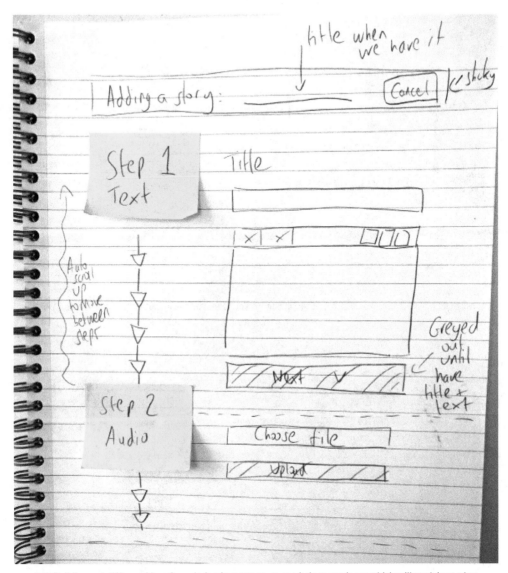

2-2. Building out different ideas for a design in a prototype can help to work out which will work best when implemented (1).

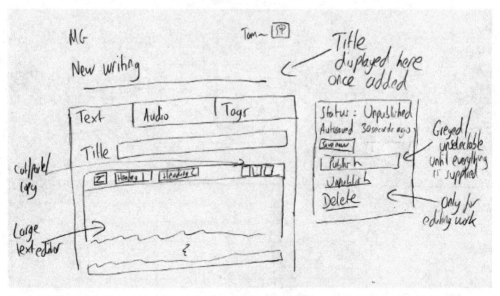

2-3. Building out different ideas for a design in a prototype can help to work out which will work best when implemented (2).

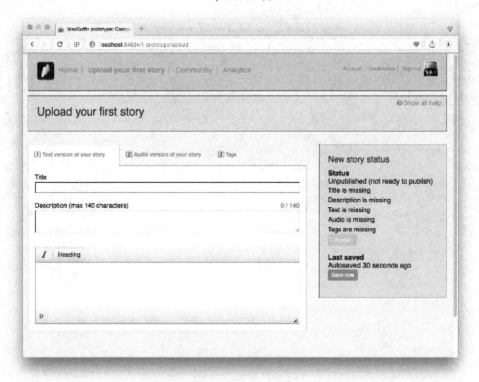

2-4. Building out different ideas for a design in a prototype can help to work out which will work best when implemented (3).

Similarly, if you're completely stuck on a design, or you feel like your ideas are terrible, the act of building a feature onscreen and have a user try it out might help you out of your design rut.

More Time Spent Communicating than Developing

If you're having to produce lots of design deliverables, then distribute, share, and explain them to others, you're probably not spending as much time as you should be actually developing your design ideas.

You might find that a simple change of approach might require resketching, revisiting the information architecture diagram, developing new wireframes, and then sharing all these changes.

A prototype can help to reduce time, effort, and pain spent updating a set of deliverables to make changes to your designs. For instance, changing the label on a navigation item and then sharing that change is trivial if it only needs tweaking in one place.

Specific Aspects of a Design Are Performing Poorly

User research might be run on an existing site, or perhaps there's tracking of analytics, measurement of conversions, or tracking of users down a sales funnel. Then the research tells you that there's a problem with a feature, or lots of users are dropping out of a conversion funnel at a specific point. Let's say you're the product manager responsible and you've been tasked with improving it.

This could be a great opportunity to take an existing implementation, come up with design ideas for improving the problematic steps, and implement them in a prototype.

Your starting point for the prototype could be a copy or basic representation of the existing scenario. Then you focus on the problematic point, explore new ideas, communicate them with the team and stakeholders, and test them with users.

Planning

A key approach when building a prototype is to get on with it (see _Get On With It!_ below). But it's a good idea to be aware of what to consider before you begin so that you start off on the right foot with the prototype. It will make the process easier and help you get the most out of it.

What are you aiming to achieve?

It's worth setting specific goals that you're trying to achieve in building a prototype. Following on from the triggers for prototyping that we've discussed, here are some examples:

- Develop the faceted navigation idea for the products page and test it with five users.
- Present the initial site structure proposal to the project team and the client's stakeholders.
- Improve conversion from the initial login step of the checkout process from 40% to 60%. Explore three UI ideas for improving this step, test it with users, and select one for further design and implementation.
- Create a prototype to demonstrate the photo-sharing concept to investors as part of our initial funding round.

Your goals will almost certainly change over time. Some will be met, others will be discarded, and often you'll need to introduce new ones. If you have your goals in mind throughout the lifetime of your prototype (that is, as you start building, when demonstrating it to a stakeholder, when sharing it, when planning and conducting a user test), you'll be better focused, and benefit more from it.

What will you test and demonstrate?

From setting your goals, you can determine early on what kind of tests to run on your prototype. It is hoped that you'll also have some user research stating some of the key goals and tasks for your users (or user groups).

Given these, you'll probably come up with a set of tasks to present to users in testing as you present and share your prototype. Try to set down these tasks in advance of building your prototype. Then, as you build, come back to your tasks to see if they are achievable. In checking tasks off your list, you'll know you're making progress and when to start testing (or retesting) with your prototype, and when to share it with your team and stakeholders, or highlight changes or additions.

Where will you place the boundaries?

You're developing a prototype, not a full-blown implementation. Given your goals, and the tasks you expect to demonstrate and test with your prototype, you're in a position to define the boundaries. You'll need to consider how much of what you're designing will be presented, and at what levels of fidelity.

If you're designing a new feature for an existing site, think about how you will present that feature within the context of the existing site. You could take a copy of the whole site including the content within it as your starting point. Then again, it may be more sensible to just recreate some of the site structure; for example, the top-level navigation in full, but lower level navigation only involving the new feature that you're designing and testing.

If you're testing a site structure, you may need to implement all the levels of that structure across the navigation. Initially, you may only need to test the primary navigation, so you're less concerned about presenting any proposed secondary navigation in the header or footer.

Think about how the prototype will behave when users reach the boundaries of what's implemented and potentially go beyond them. Users may try to access an area of the site outside the scope of the prototype, either accidentally or because they're exploring. Strategies for boundary elements (such as links and buttons) to consider here include presenting them as:

- elements with which users can interact but with no onward function; hence, if users click a link, nothing happens
- obvious placeholder content; for example, '[link to sign-up form]' so that users can see what is the next step, yet realize that they're unable to interact with it
- links to generic 'Not implemented,' 'Not ready,' or 'Not part of the prototype' content

■ links that go to a specific page but only contain placeholder content, such as a wireframe-style placeholder panel titled 'Sign-up form'

A popular approach is to initially implement widely across a prototype, but shallow. At fffunction, we implement across the range of navigation across the site structure. But we start by implementing at low fidelity with wireframe-style placeholders for modules, features, and content. Then we increase this fidelity as we design the specific areas that we want to explore, present and test with the prototype. We take a placeholder block and expand it out, break it down, and add the content it will contain. This approach suits presentation and testing of a prototype. Stakeholders and users can get a feel for the whole site and explore it, but naturally learn where the boundaries of the design are—where there's no detail and nothing to explore. This approach works more smoothly than users hitting dead ends with 'Not implemented' type messages, or the prototype breaking when users stray outside what's been implemented.

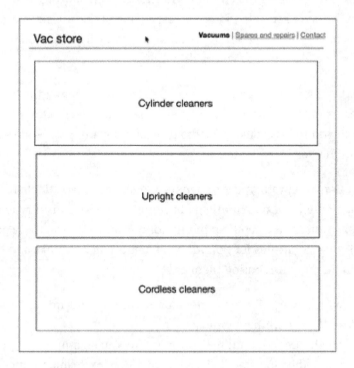

2-5. A simple clickable prototype in OmniGraffle moving into an HTML prototype, increasing fidelity as we work through designs, add detail, and obtain real content (1).

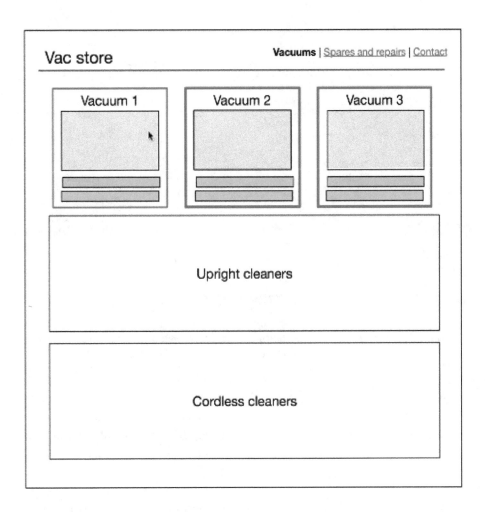

2-6. A simple clickable prototype in OmniGraffle moving into an HTML prototype, increasing fidelity as we work through designs, add detail, and obtain real content (2).

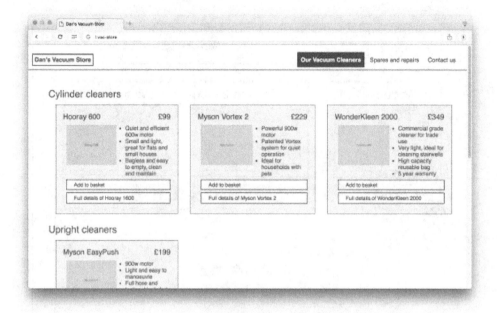

2-7. A simple clickable prototype in OmniGraffle moving into an HTML prototype, increasing fidelity as we work through designs, add detail, and obtain real content (3).

How will you use your prototype?

It's crucial to consider what you want to achieve with your prototype and how you want to share it. This will inform which prototype tools and techniques you'll employ, as well as the way you'll use them.

If you're developing and testing early-stage design ideas for yourself or with a small group of collaborators, the ability to share and demo higher fidelity prototypes may be less important. In this case, you can consider quicker, more basic tools and techniques such as paper prototyping, Keynote/Powerpoint, or a tool such as Marvel or InVision to stitch together sketches or basic mockups. These basic tools and techniques should support enough rapid user research and iteration to enable you to test and refine these early-stage ideas. We'll cover these tools and techniques in more detail later in this book.

If, however, you need to share your designs with the wider project team, or with clients, stakeholders, and third parties, tools that tend towards higher fidelity are likely to be more appropriate. They support sharing and presenting across devices in a more engaging and powerful way, but, conversely, also tend towards higher complexity and slower speeds in the creation of prototypes.

Similarly, you should think about how you conduct user research with your prototype. If you're planning on remote testing, or want users to try your prototype on their own mobile or tablet, you'll want a tool that makes it easy to create and share an online version. But if you're doing in-person research in a lab or cafe, it may be suitable to create a prototype that only runs on your own device.

Bear in mind that although you may start simple, you may require a more complicated, higher fidelity presentation later on with greater flexibility that's easier to share. You'll need to weigh up the benefits of a quicker start with basic techniques against the potential time and effort cost of switching later on. There are some tools and techniques that suit working over a wider—and changing—range of fidelities over time.

Only with experimentation and experience will you find which method will suit you and your projects best. The broad overview of the tools and techniques that we give in later chapters should help start you on the road to that experimentation.

Who will work on your prototype, and how?

You need to consider how many people are likely to be involved in your prototyping project, including in what capacity and at what point of the assignment.

If you're looking to prototype ideas in a workshop environment with multiple collaborators (perhaps including users or stakeholders), think about prototyping in a way that involves everyone quickly and easily. This would include paper prototyping, or using tools such as Marvel or InVision to link sketches and mockups together into clickable prototypes. You're unlikely to want to consume time and resources getting everyone up to speed with a bespoke prototyping tool, or by developing an HTML prototype.

Some tools and techniques (such as Keynote/PowerPoint, Axure, or OmniGraffle) may be better suited to those working in product or design management roles.

The lack of a learning curve for creating prototypes with these tools may suit them if they're already familiar with office, publishing, productivity, and basic design software and tools.

If you're working with a team of experienced web designers and developers, HTML prototyping could be a better choice. They will have plenty of experience of the technologies and processes involved, so they'll be able to contribute effectively to design ideas. They're also likely to be able to pull real content and data into a prototype, as well as process and present real user input with web development tools with which they're already familiar.

How much time, budget, and resources do you have?

If you have time, money, and resources available, you can afford to invest more in getting up to speed with a new way of working. With this scenario, you can potentially trial bespoke software and tools for a time so see if they suit your approach.

Alternatively, you might be in a situation where you're taking a risk and using your time and budget to sell the idea of prototyping where it hasn't been used before. In this case, you'll need to work as efficiently as possible, probably with limited resources. This is where you can consider cheaper and more basic approaches such as Keynote or Powerpoint, which are described in Chapter 6.

What's the starting point for your prototype?

If you (or somebody else) have already developed some design ideas with wireframes or mockups, consider using tools or techniques that enable you to use them to create interactive prototypes. Tools such as Marvel or InVision allow you to take images of sketches and wireframes (potentially at varying levels of fidelity) and quickly turn them into clickable prototypes.

If you've been given feedback on a problematic feature from a round of user tests, you may want to pick an approach that allows you to take what's there and experiment with changes to it. That might be using HTML prototyping, where you take the HTML and CSS to present a template with the current implementation before reworking to develop and test design changes. On the other hand, if the feature was developed from wireframes in a program such as Balsamiq, Keynote, or OmniGraffle, you could explore design ideas with an interactive prototype from the existing wireframes, making changes as you see fit.

Gather Resources

You'll have a better run at building a prototype if you spend time up front thinking about what resources you'll need, as well as where they'll come from.

What you need will depend on the prototyping technique you employ and the task you want to achieve with your prototype. Here is what you might need as you progress.

Existing Design Resources

Design resources in developing your prototype may include:

- relevant background information, whether it be from kickoff meetings; about the project team and stakeholders; outlining the business/organization and its goals; detailing marketing plans or audience segmentation; the project plan, timescales, and milestones
- any user research that's available, including personas or outputs from user interviews or surveys
- information architecture such as sitemaps; taxonomies; guides to labelling, terminology and language; outputs from any card-sorting exercises; or suggested navigation content, layout, and structure
- brand guidelines, visual design style guides, style tiles, or pattern libraries
- sketches and wireframes

2-8. Gather all the existing design resources that are available, such as sitemaps, brand guidelines, and insights/output from user research

Stationery (for paper prototyping)

We will discuss paper prototyping in depth in <u>Chapter 4</u>. But since we're talking about resource gathering here, what you'll need for this technique is stationery—paper, card, adhesive tape, and sticky notes—and lots of it.

Content

This could be underpinned by a documented content strategy and/or content style guides. It might include existing marketing content, or you might be able to access content from an old or existing site. If you're lucky enough to be working on a "content first" project, you may have early content around which you can design. Content that's helpful in a prototype includes labelling, navigation and taxonomies; headings; copy; images; video and other media; and download files.

As you see what content you have to use and reuse, look out for gaps of missing content, then flag these as tasks for the project team and stakeholders. You might discover that you need a copywriter working on your project.

Data

If you're working on a design that is data-driven or involves the presentation of data, having real data to work with will significantly improve the quality of your prototype. Depending on how you build your prototype, you might use data sources such as databases, APIs (application programming interfaces), CSV (comma-separated values) files, and other forms. You may be able to load and interrogate these sources, or you may have to roll your sleeves up and manually load data. Having realistic data (even if it's unofficial or less than perfect) makes a big difference to the quality, power, and usefulness of a prototype. But it can come with a price: don't underestimate the potential effort involved in finding data, moving it around, manipulating it, cleaning it up, importing it, and working with it.

An example of real data making a big difference to the quality and usefulness of a prototype is an ecommerce site. Being able to load in realistic product numbers with sufficient levels of detail (such as brands, descriptions, categories, prices, and images) makes designing and testing the site's features easier and more powerful.

id	last_name	first_name	guid
100	Wood	Kevin	28145e05-96d6-5ef8-b901-9040466757
101	Clarke	Tamara	44425a05-03ad-547e-9637-1e927f8361
102	Kane	Dueñas	2d338aa9-59d2-5a76-aef9-0b71797f22c
103	Martinez	Parker	dbbff9b5-2fbe-5ee8-9ece-a3bb4624970!
104	Lindsey	Ethel	ccb00d8c-bdf8-55a9-9d60-9d4f996fe7f7
105	Rodriquez	Carol	a9389639-4474-599e-9d4a-71c8646f9d
106	Day	Alba	fd35c8f3-30a3-5b6f-beb0-6fc02a2d18c9
107	Shamal	Juwayn	8444fbe5-b9f4-55f4-a1b0-1dac9040a0c
108	Harding	Tegan	a6c01425-bd26-56ae-a579-edb247d1b9
109	Kruse	Mathilde	94cc04dd-a4ee-50f8-a77b-d85ea45bfb3

2-9. If you can use real or sample data sets in your prototype, it will be more realistic and compelling

Get On With It!

As a section title this sounds a little flippant, but it expresses an important point with prototyping. Although you should spend some time planning your prototyping approach, avoid getting bogged down in planning and preparation.

One of the main benefits of prototyping is that it is, to some degree, quick and dirty. We should never expect to get it right first time—indeed, it would be surprising if it did. In prototyping, we should adopt a mindset where we are prepared to throw things away. Be prepared to try a tool or technique, realize when it fails to work, and throw away what you've done and try a different approach. Do the bare minimum of planning so that you're reasonably happy that you have an approach to try and then get started.

Open your tool of choice—your editor, or your pack of paper and sticky notes—and start creating.

Starting Top-down versus Bottom-up

To help decide where you'll start, use your prototype's goals and boundaries, and your ideas for how you will use and share it. If you're using a prototype to help you design specific features and elements, start to build your prototype around them. Think of this as bottom-up design.

If you're using your prototype to help inform decisions around information architecture and site structure, you'll probably be better off starting your prototype at the top levels of that structure, working down to the specific content, elements, and features. This is top-down design.

You'll probably find that you end up using a mixture of both approaches. At fffunction, we work in stages, so we use a prototype to explore initial feature design and/or structure ideas, working it up to a state where it's suitable for presenting, sharing, and testing.

Recycling Your Material

If you've been creating prototypes for a while, you probably have a collection of material to work with already. In production code, we might be cautious about copying and pasting old code to implement a new design, as it's potentially inefficient and risky. But when we're prototyping, we tend not to worry so much about reusing code, or whether it's an inefficient or inelegant way of working.

Use old projects as a starting point to get you started quickly. Throw away what you don't want, and grab, adapt, and reuse the content that you do wish to use.

None of this is to say that you should avoid working efficiently altogether. If you find yourself continually reusing the same components, create a library. And if you're copying and pasting the same group of elements over and over again, create a symbol to benefit from the "edit once, update everywhere" capability. Sketch provides a good example of using symbols—we'll discuss Sketch in Chapter 5.

Working Collaboratively

Generally, prototypes suit the collaborative working process very well. The various design skills of members on the project team can be used to best effect by working together on a prototype.

For example, someone who is responsible for information architecture can build out the top-level structure of a prototype, adding in navigation, labels, and so on. Simultaneously, another team member could be developing a user interface for a specific feature, which is then integrated into the overall structure.

Similarly, if you're working on a complicated piece of interaction design, you could set up a basic framework in which that interaction will sit, and then have different team members try out their own ideas for that interaction. You can then switch between the ideas, sharing, demonstrating, and testing them out. Then you might bring together the best aspects of the various implementations to produce the team's combined design effort.

You can work together efficiently if there's a way to give other members of the team the ability to edit content and data in your prototype. You might start by demonstrating a prototype with dummy content to a client. If they can then replace that content with real content, they can be involved in improving the fidelity of the prototype, testing out real content to see what works best in achieving the design aims.

The degree to which different prototyping methods support this kind of collaboration and integration of designs varies. Paper prototyping is very well suited to this kind of work because "integration" here means cutting and sticking pieces of paper together. If you're working in HTML, a solid collaborative workflow (such as using version control to manage everyone's code and help merge code) will make a big difference. Some tools don't easily support such collaborative working, making it difficult to work in this way. So it's another factor of which you should be aware when considering how you work.

Iterate and Demo, Testing Early and Often

Prototypes are most effective when you work quickly and share your work with your project team, stakeholders, and users as often as you can.

If you spend too long polishing a prototype to make it look amazing—populating it with loads of real content and data, and building out every element and interaction to a high degree of a detail—you miss out on the benefit of receiving feedback early and often.

Encourage your team and stakeholders to review your work as it progresses, giving feedback quickly. If you can, aim to put your work in front of users every week, or every day, or every time you finish up implementing a design idea. If you're working in sprints, test your prototype with users at the end of each one.

Summary

In this chapter, we've aimed to establish a balance between planning your prototype and getting on with building it.

We've considered some points at which you might consider using a prototype, and then we've looked at factors you should be thinking about when planning.

Finally, we've talked about the benefits of working quickly and collaboratively, iterating frequently, and demoing and testing early and often.

In the next chapter, we'll start looking at the range of prototyping tools and techniques available to use.

Chapter 3

An Overview of Prototyping Tools and Techniques

We're about to explore the various prototyping tools and approaches available (Chapters 4 to 7), but before we do, we'll use this chapter to present an overview of the landscape in which they sit.

One of the challenges we've faced while researching and writing this book is that the prototyping tools landscape is changing fast. There are several well-established tools, a swathe of tools that have emerged over the past couple of years, and new ones coming out every day. On top of that, we're seeing tool providers collaborating, competing, and buying each other out (we had to rewrite part of Chapter 5 because that very situation happened when Marvel bought POP: Prototyping on Paper while we were writing).

Another challenge we've had to grapple with is how to split the tools into meaningful groups. This is so that readers can understand the various types of tools available, as well as us being able to divide the book into sensible chapters!

We spent plenty of time reviewing how others grouped and categorized prototyping tools in other publications, blog posts, articles, and tutorials. On the whole, people tend to categorize tools by the fidelity of the prototype they produce. That's a good place to start, but we think that it's more useful to view tools in the context of more categories than fidelity alone.

Segmenting and Categorizing Tools and Techniques

We're going to build a framework comprising three groups by which to categorize prototyping tools.

Design Fidelity

If we consider different levels of fidelity, we might have a range from rapid, sketch-style prototypes, to wireframe-style prototypes that present layout up to full-fidelity design mockups that present our prototype using color palettes, typography, and other aspects of design.

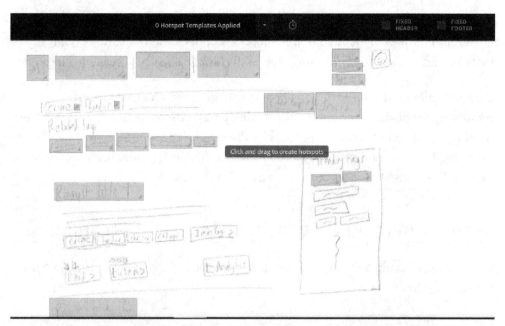

3-1. Prototypes for the search feature in MacGuffin at increasing levels of fidelity: a sketch imported into InVision (1).

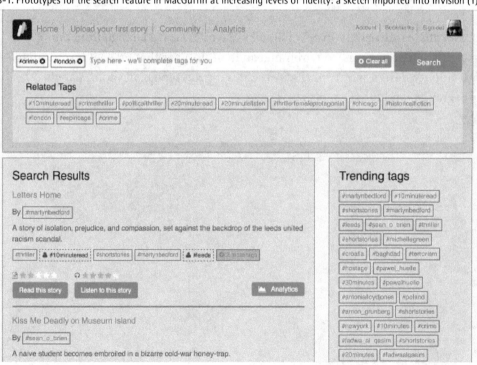

3-2. Prototypes for the search feature in MacGuffin at increasing levels of fidelity: an HTML prototype (2).

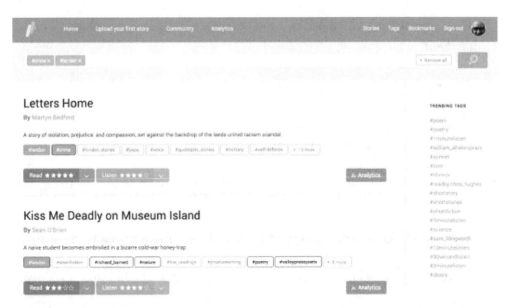

3-3. Prototypes for the search feature in MacGuffin at increasing levels of fidelity: a full-fidelity design mockup (3).

As we looked into grouping prototyping tools by fidelity, we realized there are some aspects that can make this task more complicated than one would think:

▨ There are more aspects to the fidelity of a prototype beyond the quality of visual design. These include: the level of complexity, realism, and breadth; and/or the depth of the prototype's content and navigation being presented; and the extent to which we implement user interfaces (that is, the richness and depth of interactions and whether or not transitions and animations are being presented).

▨ It's easy to conflate and confuse fidelity with complexity, difficulty, and the speed of creation of a prototype. While it's true that tools producing basic, sketch-style prototypes are typically quicker and easier to get going with, we've also noted that some more complex tools that take longer to master still only produce wireframe-level fidelity prototypes. And if you're already producing high-fidelity design mockups, some tools make turning these into high-fidelity prototypes a breeze.

▨ Many tools are capable of operating across a range of fidelities. That applies particularly to tools that take any kind of design document and enable you to produce a prototype with them (such as InVision). That document could be a sketch, a simple wireframe, or a full-fidelity design mockup. It also applies to

HTML prototypes, which can be used to create simple layout prototypes or higher-fidelity ones.

Tool Complexity and Speed of Use

Here we're considering how smoothly it is to get going with a prototyping tool. How much specialist skill and knowledge must be picked up to use a tool?

If we deliberately keep this categorization straightforward, we can split tools into three groups:

- simple to use, easy to come to grips with, and can produce prototypes fairly quickly
- complex, have a steeper learning curve, and generally take longer to produce a prototype
- lie somewhere in between

As with fidelity, it's not quite as simple as we'd like to organize prototyping tools into these categories. Here are some of the issues:

- Learning curve, speed of prototype creation, and complexity sometimes correlate, sometimes don't. Some tools and techniques have a shallow learning curve because there's simply little to learn: they're quick and simple for anyone to use. Some tools have a steep learning curve with a lot to remember, but with the payoff that once they is mastered, prototypes can be quickly created.
- Some tools naturally suit those who are comfortable working in a more technical, analytical way; other tools suit those used to working in a more design-led way; and some are a combination of both. Different people have different aptitude, skills, and experience in these approaches. Putting it another way: your mileage may vary!
- Some prototyping tools particularly suit rapid, straightforward creation of prototypes where you're already using other tools and techniques to create designs; for example, pen and paper sketching, Photoshop, or Sketch.

The Aim of Your Prototype

We've looked at various times when you might consider using a prototype in Chapter 2. In Chapter 8, we'll explore how best to use prototypes to achieve various aims in a project.

If we wanted to classify prototyping tools by aims, some categories might include to:

- rapidly generate design ideas for interfaces and user flow, and explore them
- design and present simple structures and layouts
- design and present more complex content structures and/or lengthy and involved user journeys

Sorting Tools and Techniques into Our Three Categories

We have established three ways of categorizing prototyping tools. It turns out that these can all be presented as a linear progression, with various tools sitting somewhere in that progression.

To help you better understand the range of tools we look at in this book (which reflect the wider range of tools available), we'll visualize the tools within our categories.

We're not going to attempt to map the various tools across all three categories in one diagram (well, okay, we may have actually attempted it and failed). But we can look at mappings of the tools within the three categories separately:

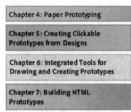

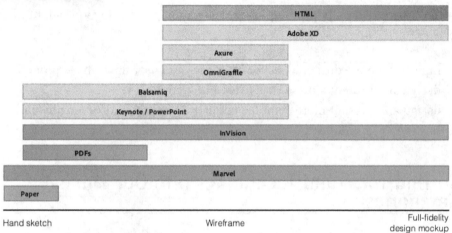

3-4. Prototype tool mapping by fidelity

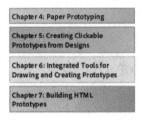

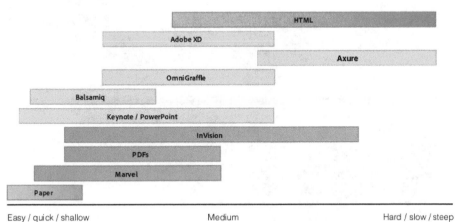

Complexity / speed of prototype creation / learning curve

3-5. Prototype tool mapping by learning curve

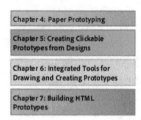

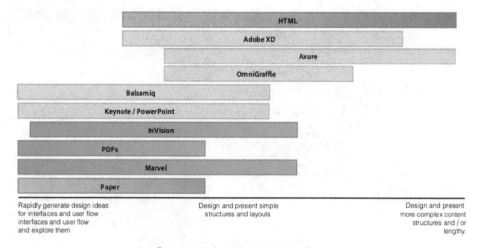

What you're using a prototype to do

3-6. Prototype tool mapping by prototype use

It's important to note that while we're reflecting a linear progression in the horizontal axis of these mappings, we aren't presenting any other progression or scale on the vertical axis. Indeed, there is no vertical axis!

It is hoped these mappings will help you to understand the prototyping tools landscape better. By looking at these mappings and working out where your projects sit, you can narrow down the set of tools and techniques to try out.

Remember that every project is unique, so you'll probably want to try different tools, techniques, and combinations with different projects that have different goals and aims, and different project and stakeholder teams.

Prototyping tools will continue to come and go, but it should be possible to consider new tools and think about where they sit within these mappings. That will help to understand when and how you can put them to best use.

Bear in mind that the three categories mapped out here will overlap to some extent and trade off against each other. Their relevance to you and your projects will apply in varying degrees. And there may well be other considerations important to you that we haven't detailed. If that's the case, you can consider mapping them out in a way that's more useful for you and your team as you learn more about them.

How the Tools Have Been Grouped

As you have already seen in figures 3-4 to 3-6, because tools sit across the various category scales we've identified and mapped out, we've split them into the following chapters:

- Chapter 4: Paper prototyping (creating prototypes from sketches on paper)
- Chapter 5: Tools for creating a clickable prototype from existing designs (including Marvel, clickable PDFs, InVision, and Powerpoint/Keynote)
- Chapter 6: Tools in which to draw and create prototypes (including Balsamiq, OmniGraffle, Axure, and Adobe XD)
- Chapter 7: HTML prototypes (using HTML and CSS code to create prototypes that run in the browser)

It's recommended that you take the time to read at least chapters 4, 5, and 6. That way, you'll be able to get a feel for the tools in those chapters that sit across our mappings: fidelity, complexity, and tasks. We feel that anybody involved in the design of websites and web apps will find tools and techniques enabling them to create prototypes straight away.

If you feel that you're "technically challenged", you might have the preconception that HTML prototyping is beyond your abilities. But with the support of some more technically minded project team members and a little effort, you may find you can still reap the benefits of HTML prototyping in terms of flexibility and value. So we'd urge everyone to read Chapter 7 too.

Tools that Failed to Make the Cut

There are *loads* of tools that can be used to create prototypes. It is hoped that we've considered most of them to a degree as we researched and wrote this book. But we're aware there are tools that we don't even know about. And, as mentioned, some tools will fall out of favor, go out of production, and be bought out or assimilated into other tools. And we know that new tools are coming out all the time and will continue to do so.

This is why we've provided a framework to help you evaluate various tools from a range of perspectives, so that you can establish whether you're likely to find them useful.

There are some specific tools that didn't quite make it into the book. This is because:

- they're more suited to prototyping native applications (we're deliberately focusing on tools for prototyping websites and web apps in this book).
- they don't easily fit into the structures of categories and chapters we've established.
- they're arguably more technical- and developer-oriented than the intended core audience for the book
- it's down to a simple lack of time and space.

We've briefly covered the following tools in Appendix A:

- Craft by InVision
- Facebook Origami Studio
- Framer
- Principle
- Xcode

Summary

In this short chapter, we've attempted to map the prototyping tools landscape by coming up with three sets of categories into which the tools can be mapped: fidelity, complexity, and tasks.

We've shown that the various tools available sit in ranges across linear progressions of these three categories. And we've encouraged you to consider combinations of these categories and the tools within them to suit you and your projects.

We've also noted that there are many more prototyping tools than those we've written about here, and that the landscape is changing fast with new tools emerging (and disappearing) all the time. We've explained how you can consider new tools in the context of categories——ours and others——to work out whether they're likely to be useful.

In the next chapter, we're going to start by looking at one of the simplest and yet most powerful prototyping tool sets: paper!

Chapter

4

Paper Prototyping

In this chapter, we take a look at paper prototyping. We'll cover what it entails, and its pros and cons. We'll cover what's required for paper prototyping, and present different examples on how to create and use prototypes.

What is paper prototyping?

Paper prototyping is the act of making prototypes out of paper-based material. It might be paper, card, cardboard, notebooks, sticky notes, or other forms of the medium—anything you can cut, fold, draw on, and adapt to become a prototype that once may have been a tree.

Paper prototyping predates the Internet. Designers developed it in the 1980s to help them create software. Nowadays, it's used across a range of design disciplines.

Paper prototyping can improve a project's outcome, while also saving time and money. It's the form of prototyping with the lowest barrier to entry, so it's the most inclusive.

In his book *Designing Interactions*[1], Bill Moggridge advised "Prototype early and often." Using paper offers you a great opportunity to prototype early in the design process. It's also rapid enough to enable you to do it frequently.

> "By prototyping early and often, each iterative step becomes a little more realistic. At some point you are likely to experience that wonderful "Aha!" feeling that comes with a creative leap, but bear in mind it only indicates you have progressed in the detail of the aspect of the design on which you are currently focusing. You will only know the design is good once you have tried it out with those who will use it, and found that they are pleased, excited, and motivated with the result."

Paper prototyping during the creative process can help you generate ideas, singly or collaboratively, and try them out. It fosters understanding with clients and your project team by enabling you to show them an idea. You can also test designs with users for validating and refining.

Let's look at the pros and cons of using paper prototyping.

Pros

Test Ideas Quickly

Because it's the most rapid form of prototyping, you can obtain user feedback as early as possible in the design process. You can generate a prototype for testing, and make changes quickly based on the outcomes of those tests.

[1.] http://www.designinginteractions.com/book

Cheap and Involves No Tools or Training

All that's required are common everyday items with which everyone is familiar. There are no hard and fast rules about how to create them, so no training is required. Some tips are always useful to guide the way, though (more on that later!).

Particularly Suited to Collaborating

Anyone and everyone can be involved in a hands-on activity that benefits the project in many ways. It's fun, it helps build relationships, and it engages and involves the client in the design process in the best way possible.

Creating a Shared Understanding

In any project, creating and maintaining a shared understanding is critical. Talking about an idea or writing a specification while useful, won't rule out others failing to understand the whole picture. They might still have a slightly or completely different idea in their heads. By showing the offering with a sketch or paper prototype, you can create a shared understanding of an idea that may be later refined, rejected, or tested with users.

No Training Necessary

Everyone can draw to some degree, but sometimes they need a little encouragement. Tips can help, but there is no right or wrong way to create a paper prototype. From novices to experts, everyone can get involved.

No Technical Constraints

Unlike other prototyping methods, you are not limited by technical constraints.

With paper, you are only restrained by your imagination and the physical items you can use. Want to invent new ways of controlling an interface? This is the quickest way to do it, enabling you to draw, cut, and affix new elements faster than any other method.

Cons

It's Unresponsive

The nature of paper prototyping is that you need to identify what you're designing for. It's best to take an adaptive approach and choose phone, tablet, or desktop as a starting point for a prototype.

Once you've created a phone-orientated paper prototype, for example, you could then go and create a desktop version with more features. Doing so could develop the basis of a good responsive design system; however, you wouldn't be able to do it in the same manner as, say, an HTML prototype. Nor is it easy to do anything else that depends on a responsive prototype, such as distribute to different viewports or conduct remote testing.

Lots of Stationery Required

You need lots of paper, pens, sticky dots, mounting putty such as Blu Tack, sticky notes, and so on. This takes time to organize: sourcing and ordering the materials, and then transporting them if you're traveling.

Needs Supervising

Once created, how do you make a paper prototype work? Often it involves physically handling the paper based on the test participant's interactions, so you need to be there in person *working* the prototype. You can, however, digitize or make paper prototypes clickable, which we'll cover in the next chapter.

Takes Practice and Experience to Run Research Sessions

Running a user research session requires a decent amount of organization and practice to ensure it's a seamless experience for the user. Lots of paper shuffling is involved and you need to know exactly what you're doing for each interaction the user makes. Any disruption could have a negative impact on the session's effectiveness. As with the previous point, you can also deal with this issue by digitizing your prototype.

Not Easy to Share

You have to physically move paper or take pictures of everything, stitch it together and then share. You can make paper prototypes distributable (covered in Chapter 8), but this should be a consideration when you choose which prototyping method to use.

Difficult to Edit

Making changes can often mean starting again; for instance, it's tricky to change text once it's been added. You can cut and stick more paper to make alterations, but there's a point where further refinement of a prototype should be completed in a digital medium. The upside is that if you are forced to redraw some detail, you are also forced to review and reflect on it, and often the second version will be better.

Making Paper Prototypes

There are no rules for making paper prototypes—that is what's great about it. You need materials that are commonly found in any home or office, but if you have to buy them, they are relatively inexpensive.

What You'll Need

At the very least you'll require paper and a pen—this low barrier to entry is one of the best aspects about this approach. For more complex and interactive prototypes, though, you'll need a bigger arsenal, and if you're running workshops or doing a lot of prototyping, assembling a toolkit of the following items is a good idea.

We'd suggest the following items when undertaking a prototyping session:

- paper with a grid or dot grid (preferred)
- sticky notes (never leave home without them!)
- pencils
- eraser
- pens (Sharpies in different colors and thicknesses are ideal)

- scissors or craft knife
- glue (preferably restickable)

Items that are nice to have include:

- index cards
- mounting putty
- adhesive tape (preferably removable to move items around)
- highlighter pens
- double-ended marker pens with fine and normal nibs
- transparent sheets and markers
- a box for filing or transporting your prototype

We'll look at the possibilities involved in using different materials later in the chapter.

Your Approach

Strictly speaking, you could just dive in and start making; however, a process we've found helpful at fffunction is to think outward-in, focusing on increasingly smaller pieces as you go, such as:

1. devices
2. screens
3. elements
4. interactivity or state changes

Devices

What size viewport or device are we designing for in this instance? Any available user research may inform this. Analytics data will indicate what an existing audience may prefer to use. A goal of the design work could be to prototype an improved experience on small-screen devices.

Desktop or Laptop

An A4- or US letter-sized piece of paper is suitable here, where you could use different orientations to mimic the device, such as landscape for a desktop or laptop. If you want a more realistic source, you could print out a browser frame graphic.

Tablet

A5- or US half-letter-sized paper should suffice, although if you're designing for a large tablet such as the Apple iPad Pro (12.9 inches), you might want to stick with the A4/Letter size. Again, you can choose an orientation depending on what you expect the user to have. If you want to make this more realistic, creating a dummy device is an option. The most lo-fi approach would be to draw it on a piece of card and cut out a hole where the screen would be, as depicted below.

4-1. A simple iPad model made from cardboard

Laser-cut and 3D-printed devices have been created specifically to help use paper prototypes in a more natural way, allowing the prototype to be part of a device.

Phone

As with the previous examples, you can sketch directly onto paper: A5- or US half-letter-sized, index cards, or sticky notes, and use different orientations. There are more options available for mobile devices, though, than any other form.

You could make a cellphone border with a cutout window for the screen, or use cards laid on top of the device to act as different screens.

As mentioned, there are also laser-cut and 3D-printed device models available. The figure below shows a laser-cut plywood phone model that we use in our work.

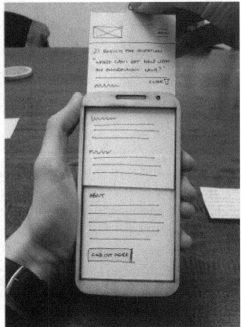

4-2. Laser-cut device with paper inserts

Plastic or card model devices with a channel to insert pieces of paper to simulate scrolling are also available. You could even place all the screens on a long piece of paper and slide it around to simulate navigation.

Another option is to use a small spiral-bound notebook to flick between screens, with tabs or colored dots forming navigation elements, as seen below. This is a nice approach as it mimics how people use their cellphone: held in one hand while the other taps it to interact.

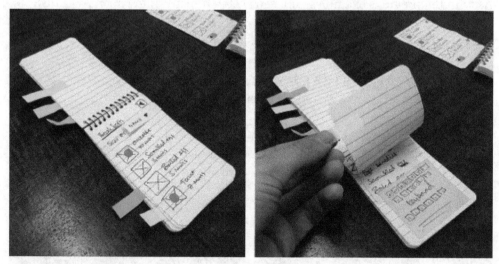

4-3. A notebook prototype

Screens

Now we'll define what screens are required to communicate the design. It's helpful to consider what steps in the journey the user will take. We can develop a list from existing work such as user journeys, task models, sitemaps, information architecture, or a functional specification. Some of this was covered in the _Gather Resources_ section of Chapter 2, to which you can refer back if you need a refresher. Once you've developed a list, you can start to think about what elements will be required for each screen.

If you don't know the screen size, or have an incomplete picture of what you are designing, sketching the steps out on cards can be useful for working a product at a high level before going into more detail. We'd recommend beginning with smaller A5 or index cards to help you focus on the individual interactions on each screen; aiming for one purpose per screen is a good way to start. You can then arrange them on a table to experiment with different flows through a process.

Elements

When looking at the elements that make up your screen, consider how users will interact with them during the prototype process. What needs to happen when they touch that element?

In some cases, you may have a consistent interface with only one window changing based on interactions around it. A simple example would be a menu in a left-hand column that changes the content of the right-hand column. This could be represented with the same card on the left, and separate cards for each piece of interchangeable content on the right, as shown below.

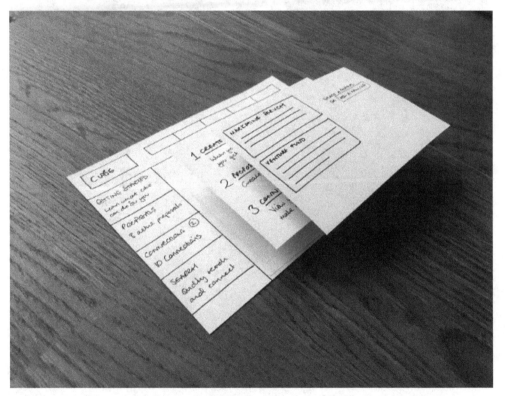

4-4. A screen showing fixed and interchangeable content

Interactivity

All the elements you've established will each be interactive at various points. There's a challenge here in how to replicate that functionality with paper. Again, there's likely to be no "right first time" solution to this so it's worth experimenting with different materials and approaches.

Scrolling and sliding

One approach we've used is to cut parts out of the screen and then threading strips of paper through to enable sliding and scrolling elements. A 1–2 mm hole is large enough to slip paper through and enable the right amount of clearance for "scrolling." The figure below depicts a paper vertical scrolling device.

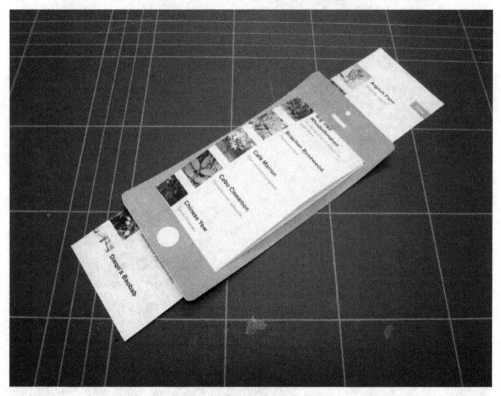

4-5. Vertical scrolling device

Another approach is to use a more advanced device model with a slot to slide paper through indicating a horizontal scroll.

4-6. Horizontal scrolling device

Menus

For a menu, pieces of paper can be placed into position on an interaction, or, similarly, you could use sticky notes so that they hold their position but are easy to move.

If you're using a cutout device, the menu could be positioned off the canvas or out of sight, then slid in to be revealed as depicted below.

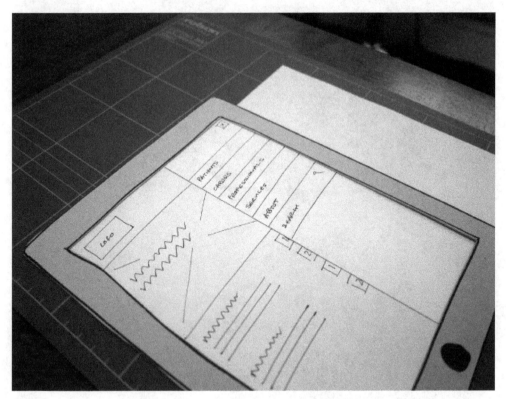

4-7. A menu shown off-canvas but ready for revealing

Messages and Pop-up Boxes

Sticky notes are handy for messages, popups, or tooltips as they can be placed on the screen and then removed following an interaction or after a period of time. You can purchase them in smaller sizes, even speech bubble shapes that are perfectly suited to this as shown below.

4-8. Sticky note speech bubbles are ideal for messages or popups

Tabs

You can either create your own tabs by cutting them out of paper, or buying index cards. When selecting another tab, shuffle through the deck of tab cards and arrange the selected tab on top.

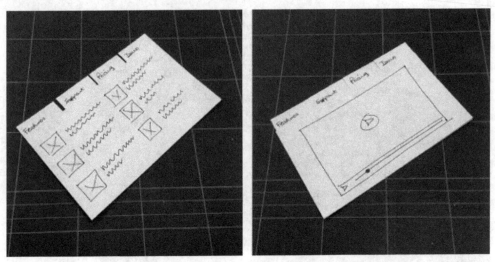

4-9. Paper or index cards easily substitute for tabs

Accordions

Now's the time for a little origami. Draw the accordion content with everything in view on the page. Starting at the top, fold up the accordion so that just the titles are visible and the drawer content is hidden. Then, when you tap on a title, you can reveal the folded piece of content. The figure below presents this process.

If you'd prefer to skip the folding you could make individual pieces, or use sticky notes for the sections that will be revealed.

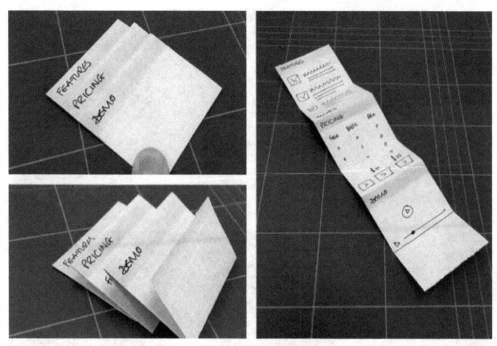

4-10. Bending it like ... an accordion

A common responsive design pattern is to interchange an accordion style menu on smaller screens with tabs on larger screens. You can see this prototyped as two distinct elements in the figure below.

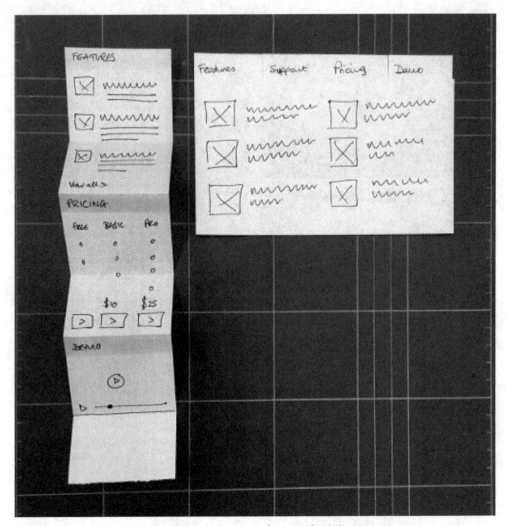

4-11. Accordion and tabs as part of a responsive design pattern

Slide Up / Down Reveals

The techniques that we've already covered can be employed here. You could elect to hide the content off canvas, or slide it in to view from a slit in the paper. Or you could simply place the content on a separate card and lay it into place when required.

Select Boxes

Sticky notes work well here to depict a moveable list of items that you would see in a select element, as shown below. The user will be able to see the choices and select one, at which point you can remove the list from the prototype.

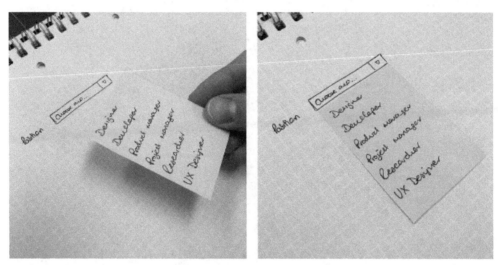

4-12. A select box using a sticky note for a drop-down menu

Checkboxes and Radio Buttons

Simply drawing these often suffices for a prototype. You could go as far as to place checked versions on top of the unchecked version following an interaction.

If part of the purpose of the prototype is to experiment with the positioning of elements on a page, a strip cut of a sticky-note would work.

You have to weigh up the complexity of building and operating this element in a test scenario against the benefits of having the detail. Make it too fiddly and operating your prototype will become difficult.

iOS / Android Native Design Elements

There's the option of adding complicated design elements from iOS or Android that could be tricky to replicate or take time to sketch. For example, to reproduce a calendar, it's simpler to take a screenshot of one from a device, then print and cut it out, rather than sketch it.

You could elaborate on this and print out a stencil or toolkit library for a device, should you think it will speed up the process and not make the design too prescriptive.

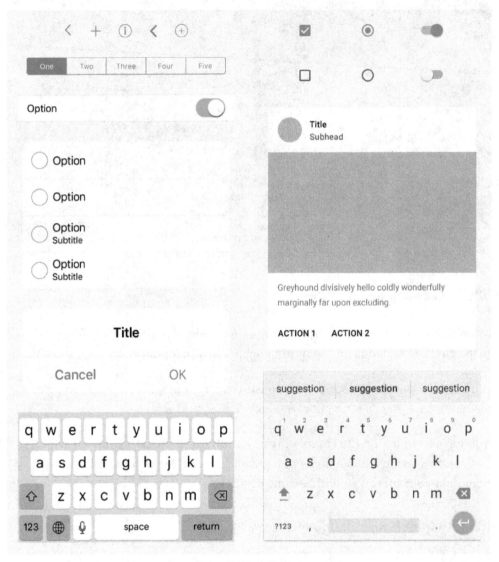

4-13. Native elements

Literally *Anything*

The aforementioned examples are common design elements that can be found on a standard website, tablet, or phone, but there's no reason to be constrained by what you've seen before. As has been mentioned, one of the pros of paper prototyping is that you're not bound by the constraints of a digital medium. If you can imagine it, you can probably make it out of paper and prototype with it.

Drawing Tips

When creating paper prototypes, you'll need to draw elements to make up your sketches. In some circumstances, you may not have to spell out content or be particularly detailed about the elements you're laying onto the page. This could be because you're focusing the interaction on a certain module or element, and want to avoid any distraction with other elements.

In this scenario, you can utilize a sketching shorthand to represent common elements. As depicted below, titles can be wavy lines, paragraph text with straight lines, and images boxes with diagonal lines across them as you would see in a wireframe.

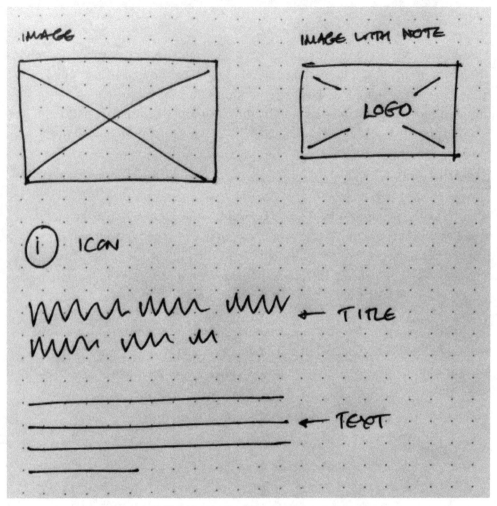

4-14. Sketching shorthand tips for paper prototypes

Of course this ignores another pro of using paper prototyping compared to wireframes. Wireframes use a box with diagonal lines to represent an image. You might label a box to indicate what it is, but unless you add an image, your communication is fairly limited. In sketching, you can explore further and sketch the actual content of the image. In the figure below we're introducing a new product by sketching a hero image with two customers using the product. This provides the user with a rough approximation of the experience with the final design.

4-15. A hero image sketch showing customers using the product

Paper Prototypes from Digital Files

We've seen designers use an application to create digital designs or wireframes, and then print them out to use as a paper prototype. This could be because they have a lot of assets available digitally in a style guide or pattern library. Or they feel they can work just as fast on a computer as with stationery and the tools mentioned.

These digital designs are still low-fidelity wireframes, having been printed out and cut up into the component parts required to make the prototype function in a testing environment. The manipulation of screens and elements, addressed later in the chapter, is still the same as if they were handmade.

We'd argue that the time taken to do this could be better spent turning those designs into a clickable prototype, rather than a paper one, as they already exist in that medium. We'll cover making prototypes clickable in the next chapter.

Collaboration = Team + Client + Users

Paper prototypes are an excellent way of bringing collaboration into the design process. They enable a shared understanding among the whole project team of what is being designed. Clients will see the direction being taken early on in the design process, and it also brings visual designers and developers into the design process earlier than might otherwise be the case.

Collaborative Creation of Prototypes

Paper prototypes can be created collaboratively by running a workshop with clients and/or users. The purpose of these workshops is to rapidly generate, discuss, and select ideas with which to progress.

To run a prototyping workshop, you need an idea of the users' goals. From there, think about the situation they might be in, the device they are using, and so on. Then you need to work out the steps users follow to perform the task being prototyped. You can also refer to an existing website or information architecture to help decide what will form the prototype.

The number of participants can influence how you approach the workshop. Individuals could create prototypes on their own and then come together to present and discuss their ideas. Or the group could prototype as one and then use role-playing to validate the prototype. If there's enough people, you could split a particularly long user journey in two and have a team approach each half, or have two teams tackle the one scenario so that there are two prototypes to compare.

Materials for a Prototyping Workshop

- paper or card
- assorted pens for drawing, coloring, and highlighting
- adhesive putty
- scissors (safer than knives)

- sticky notes
- adhesive tape
- glue sticks
- sticky dots for voting
- timer (watch or cellphone will suffice)

Outlining the Purpose

Arm everybody with paper and a pen. Select a user journey or task to prototype and discuss what the user is trying to do, and what the system you are prototyping requires.

Ready, Steady, Go!

Once everyone understands the brief, start the timer, and get going. A decent amount of time to allow for a simple prototype is 10 to 15 minutes.

 Marking the Playing Field

A wide-tipped marker such as a Sharpie is recommended to level the artistic playing field when drawing or sketching. Some people draw beautifully, others don't, and we wouldn't want that to affect participation rates, or voting and decision-making. A wide tip means that the sketches will look similar in quality, although the content can vary widely.

Presenting and Testing Ideas

Your approach to presenting each idea will depend on how many people are in the workshop, and whether they work individually or in teams.

Individuals might demonstrate their prototype to the group and explain their thinking, while teams might benefit from presenting their prototype as in a user-testing scenario. If a prototype was designed collectively, role-playing is a great way to validate it.

Role-playing a prototype works by assigning two people to perform distinct roles. One should be the device, and the other, the user. Each acts out their side of any interactions or decisions they make. They narrate their thought processes as they go, enabling the rest of the group to understand what is happening. By exploring the user journey this way, you'll quickly see where there might be issues with the prototype and ways to improve it.

Voting

A voting system will enable you to narrow the selection of ideas and work out what to include in a prototype. This is where the sticky dots come in. Give each participant a handful of dots and ask them to place a dot on each idea—or part of an idea—that they think should be included in the prototype. More than one dot can be added to an idea if it *really* needs to be part of the prototype.

Workshop Outcomes

There should now be a selection of ideas with a clear indication as to what elements of each should be utilized in the design process. The next step could be to take the ideas into a user-testing phase to validate them with real users.

There may be a need for some refinement before ideas are progressed. Ideas for a template design may come from multiple prototypes, for example, or they might be too low a fidelity to be used for testing. They could be reworked, or even taken forward in a digital medium.

Variants on this Approach

Another approach could be to assign different parts of a prototype to people in the team. An information architect may be well-suited to creating a navigation system, while a content writer could produce actual content for the page, and so on.

"Responsifying" an Existing Site with Paper Collage

At fffunction, some of our work has entailed a client coming to us with the goal of making their existing website responsive. They've invested a lot in their site, and are happy with the way it looks, behaves, and works for their organization, but it was designed and built without being responsive. Often they've identified this as being a barrier to their users completing certain tasks on the site, some even having analytics data to back this up. In essence they need their site *responsifying.*

So, how do we approach this? There's an existing design, but we could sketch new layouts, or we could create new wireframes to define what happens on smaller screens. As there are already elements to play with, we can use them to collage a new design for smaller screens. By printing out the web pages, cutting them up, and sticking them back together again, we can make decisions about layout, visual hierarchy, and interactive elements. You can do this alone, or collaboratively with your team and your client.

Screen Capture

The first hurdle is to print the site in its screen form. Most sites will have a print stylesheet that presents the site's content in a print-friendly format. We'll need to capture the site's in-browser format, which can be done using a browser extension for Chrome called Awesome Screenshot[2]. The important feature is being able to capture the full site page rather than just the visible portion of the page. Once that's done, we have a flat image file of our page—and if it's possible, a PDF format is even better.

Printing and Converting to PDF for Large Images

We want to print out each page so that we can cut it up to produce a collage. Enter the world of pain that is print settings: longer pages will be shrunk to fit on a single page, which can make the elements too small to use, as you can (almost) see below.

[2.] https://www.awesomescreenshot.com

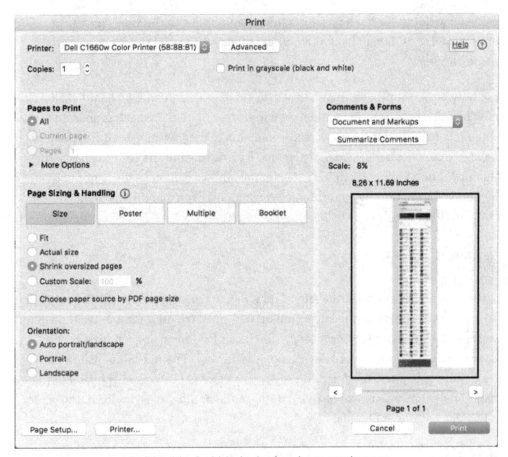

4-16. Print dialog for Adobe Acrobat featuring an extra long page

The solution is to create a PDF from this image using an app such as Preview or Acrobat. Using Adobe Acrobat's poster mode, you can then print it over several pages at a similar size at which you would see it on screen, as shown below.

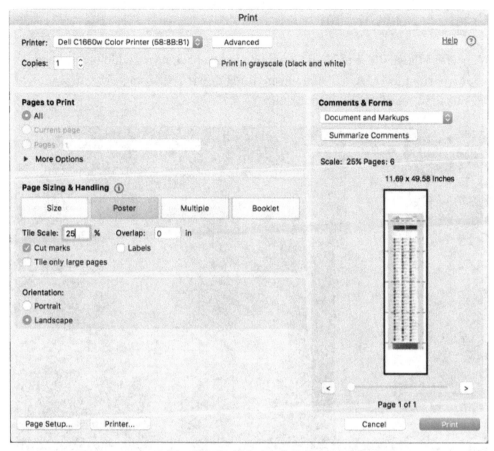

4-17. Print dialog for Adobe Acrobat in Poster mode

Slicing and Dicing

Once printed, cut up the site into modules or elements. It can help to sketch lines around elements or groups of elements, so think about grouping items that belong together. For example, the metadata of a blog post that includes the author's name, published date, and post category might appear together on the image, so consider these elements forming a group that can be cut out as one piece.

Once you've decided on your element groups, start cutting the page up into pieces.

Creating a New Design

Now grab a large piece of blank paper to use as a backing on which to arrange your website pieces. Avoid sticking anything down at this stage, as you want to be able to move pieces around to suit.

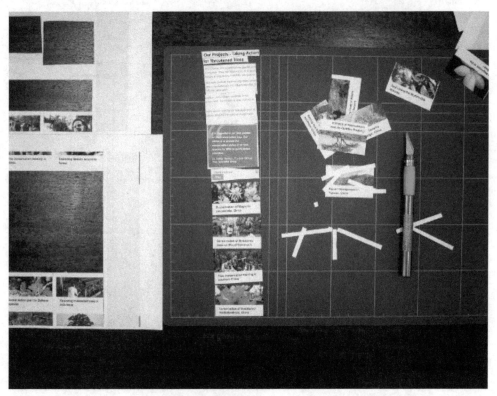

4-18. Cut pieces being re-assembled

Consider also whether the elements need to be edited. For example, focusing more on an image's subject so that it's not lost when displayed at a smaller size, and removing part or all of an element that's not required on smaller devices.

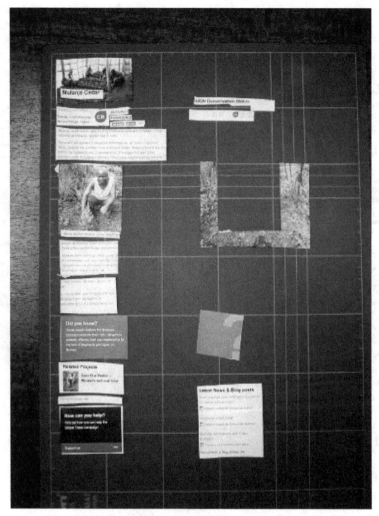

4-19. Editing and removing elements

Once you've worked out what to use, stick the elements in place to create a collage. Adhesive putty or removable magic tape is best here as you may still want to rearrange elements.

4-20. Assembling your collage

Sketching the Gaps

You may find that your collection of cutouts doesn't quite cut it with your design aims when putting together your collage. In some cases, what you've cut out just won't work on smaller screens, or might be too fiddly to stick into place. There could also be a change in interface or functionality for smaller screens that you wish to make. At this point, you could sketch the new element to fit into the design—either on a new piece of paper so that you can still move it around, or onto the backing paper, as shown below.

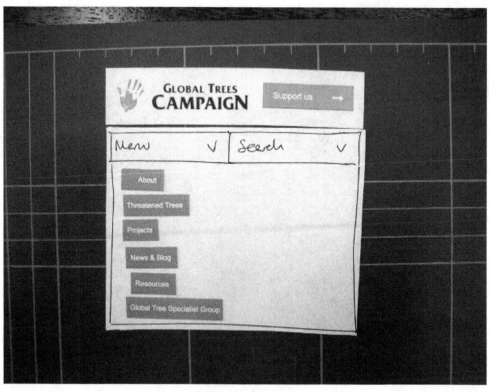

4-21. Sketching new elements for a prototype

The Finished Article

You should now have a finished collage of what the site could look like on a smaller screen, such as shown below. Use this to focus discussions on the responsive version of the site with project stakeholders, as well as to guide designers and developers in implementing these changes.

4-22. A responsive collage

There are some areas for which this method may be unsuitable. A good example is the main navigation of the website. It is common for navigation to look very different on small devices compared to large screens. There are also some instances where you will have a complete change in functionality for smaller screens.

In these cases, wireframing or referring to an existing design pattern is probably a better option.

Paper Prototypes in Use

Now that we've covered the creation of prototypes, let's look at how you'd *use* a prototype. There are several reasons for creating one so lets look at each in turn.

Presenting Ideas and Soliciting Feedback

If you need to present a design to an audience from different backgrounds, a prototype can help explain the ideas you are trying to get across. It's a rapid way of creating something physical to communicate the idea that anyone can use it and get a feel for it.

A benefit to the low-fidelity nature of this is that people are less afraid to contribute feedback. It facilitates discussion, where together you can iterate the ideas presented and push the prototype further, as it's quick to amend existing or create new pieces. It can also avoid unhelpful feedback that focuses on the wrong level of fidelity; for example, debate brand colors or typography when you want to work on flow and interaction at this stage.

Testing the Prototypes with Users

In most cases, the purpose of creating a prototype is to test it with real users. This validates the ideas behind the prototype and exposes potential issues with the design.

As Jakob Nielsen said[3], "Five users should be able to identify about 85% of all usability problems." A lot of discussion exists about how many users you should test with, but as an initial guide five is a good number, as the law of diminishing returns attests below. So find some users and you're ready to start testing.

[3.] https://www.nngroup.com/articles/why-you-only-need-to-test-with-5-users/

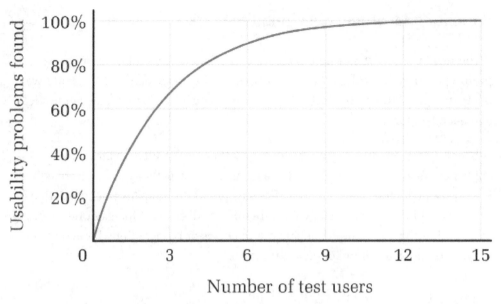

4-23. User testing diminishing returns chart

Roles in the Test Session

In order to run prototype test sessions, several people need to fulfill certain roles:

Facilitator Facilitators run the session. It's their job to explain what is going on to the user and set them at ease. Facilitators reassure users that they are not under any pressure to respond a certain way, nor are responsible for the prototype.

Facilitators give the users scenarios or tasks to complete and gently remind them as to their motivations and goals. They must on no account help the user though—that's cheating, and would reduce the usefulness of the test.

Operator / Human Computer Operators, well, operate the prototype. They need to be very organized, and know about all the elements and possible interactions of the prototype. When a user interacts with the prototype, the operator needs to move elements around and shuffle pages, imitating the results of that interaction. To run the session smoothly is quite a challenge, so they must be familiar with all the options and know where everything is.

User   Users are asked to interact with the prototype. They are presented with a scenario in which they have a specific task or goal that they then attempt to carry out using the prototype. Users should be encouraged to verbalize their train of thought in order to understand their decisions.

Observer   Observers watch the session and takes notes on the users' interactions with the prototype. These notes will be used to refine the prototype and iron our any issues uncovered by the testing. Observers can be in the room, or in another location watching the interaction via video.

Anatomy of a Test Session

With these people in place you're now ready to run a session. Let's look at how that works.

The facilitator explains to the user what the aim of the test session is, and the roles of everyone present. It should be made clear that there are no wrong outcomes, and the user should be made to feel at ease.

The user is then given their first scenario or task to attempt. Users can point at an element to mimic a touch interaction, or they might use a pen or pencil so that their actions are more evident to the observer, operator, and camera if the session is being recorded.

If you've used the spiral notebook approach, the facilitator will need to explain the premise of the notebook and how to navigate the reference tabs. There's also the challenge of recording this particular approach, accounting for the various sizes of users and how they differ in holding the notebook.

The user then moves through each scenario, completing the tasks while the observer takes notes on actions performed. These notes can then be used to improve the prototype.

Once a user has run through all the scenarios, they are then asked by the facilitator for their thoughts on the prototype—its good points and bad. Did the user experience any problems at any stage? The aim is to explore their experience in more detail. The final output of the user sessions should be a list of issues and actions to progress the design and improve the prototype.

Digitizing Paper Prototypes

We mentioned previously that some of the disadvantages of paper prototypes are that they cannot work on their own, and that they are hard to share at a distance or test with users remotely. Fortunately, there are ways around this, and we'll cover the techniques of digitizing an item that is not by nature a shareable electronic artefact in the next chapter.

Summary

In this chapter, we've covered what a paper prototype is and the various methods there are for making them.

We've also considered some different use cases for paper prototyping including testing with users, co-designing with a prototyping workshop, and "responsifying" a site with collage techniques.

It's fast, it's cheap, it's good—so have a go now!

In the next chapter, we'll look at how you can digitize paper prototypes and make them clickable.

Chapter

5

Creating Clickable Prototypes from Designs

In this chapter, we'll take a look at prototyping tools that are a step up from basic paper prototyping.

These tools enable us to take a set of flat designs of some kind and stitch them together to create a prototype that is *clickable*. This is more powerful and engaging for stakeholders, team members, and users because:

- there's no need for us to drive the prototypes, switching paper templates and sketches in and out as users interact with them
- the prototype is more responsive, realistic, and immersive.
- it can work standalone, enabling us to share it remotely. The people we've shared the prototype with can test it on their own, at their own pace and—dependent on the tool—using a range of their own devices.

A flat design with which these tools can operate is anything that can be captured as a digital image, such as:

Sketches
Some tools in this category (for example, Marvel) support using a mobile device to take pictures of sketches, then adding **hotspots** to stitch them together into a clickable prototype. Using sketches in this way bridges the gap perfectly between simple paper prototyping and higher-fidelity techniques.

Wireframes and user interface designs
These typically present the layout of content and/or user interface elements in our designs; indeed, they could be regarded as higher-fidelity versions of a sketch. There are a variety of existing tools and methods to create such designs, such as Sketch, Balsamiq, Keynote/PowerPoint, OmniGraffle, or Photoshop. Regardless of what you use, if you can save flat images of your designs, you can build a prototype with them.

Higher-fidelity mockups
Higher-fidelity design comps or mockups created in Photoshop or with other design tools can be used to create prototypes. As we've already discussed in Chapter 1, this is not the most cost-effective way of working since the cost of implementing and changing designs increases with fidelity. Nevertheless, you may find yourself in a situation where you have high-fidelity mockups already prepared, and you can gain more value by using them to create a prototype.

We'll start by discussing perhaps the simplest of the techniques that is one step up from paper prototyping: using a basic tool to turn sketches and paper prototypes into a clickable form.

 From POP to Marvel

Until recently, many folks used an app called POP (Prototyping on Paper) to turn sketches into a prototype. As we were writing this book, Marvel bought POP and retired the POP app. Marvel does what POP does—and more, hence why we discuss Marvel here.

Marvel

Marvel is a prototyping tool that is growing rapidly—in terms of maturity and feature set, and in terms of popularity. Similar to InVision (discussed later on), it can be used to create prototypes by importing design files of any kind and adding hotspots to them. It also includes design and drawing functionality so you can design layouts in the application itself (also the case with the tools we discuss in Chapter 6). In fact, it's a powerful and flexible prototyping powerhouse!

We're featuring it here because as well as being a fully featured, flexible web-based application, there are also native iOS and Android apps that support the rapid creation of prototypes on phones and tablets from sketches. As such, Marvel is—at the time of writing—the best example of an app that simplifies the process of taking pictures, adding hotspots, and linking them together to produce a clickable prototype on one device.

Here's a typical process for creating a prototype:

1. Start with a series of sketches you've come up with for a design problem. It works better if the sketches are all the same size and have same aspect ratio (that is, they're all landscape or all portrait). When you start a Marvel project using the mobile app, you have to select an aspect ratio and viewport size; this differs from using the web application on a desktop or laptop).
2. Take pictures of your sketches with your mobile device to create prototype screens. You can do this in the Marvel app, or you can use your device's camera (which gives you more control over capturing and editing your pictures) and then import them in from your image gallery. Each image becomes a screen in your prototype.
3. Add one or more linked hotspots to a screen that, when tapped, will move to another screen, as shown below. A range of transitions between screens are supported, such as fade, push left, slide left, and slide up.
4. Hit **Play** to run the prototype you've created on the device. You could use this as a demo for your team and stakeholders, or hand it to a user to step through and test your prototype.

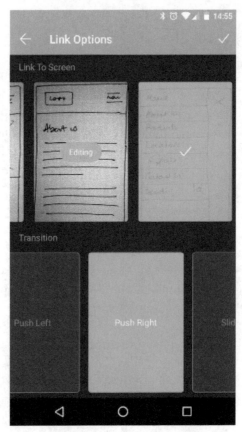

5-1. Adding a hotspot to link a page to another page in a sketch-based prototype that is created on an Android phone using Marvel

And that's really it!

On desktops or laptops, you'll have to create a user account to use the web-based app. If you sign in to the mobile app with your user account, you can sync your prototypes between devices and the cloud or the web app. This means that they're backed up; you can share them with other Marvel users in your team for potential collaboration; and you can share the prototype through a URL with stakeholders for reviews, demos, and user research.

Marvel further supports creating prototype screens by drawing on devices. You can use your fingers or, with the relevant hardware, a stylus.

The Marvel desktop/laptop web app also supports creation of prototypes by importing images or designs from other design tools, or by syncing them using

Dropbox or Google Drive. But if you're using these features, you're moving beyond the simple paper sketch-based workflow we're discussing here.

Using Marvel to create prototypes from sketches makes sense in a situation where you're already sketching out your designs, whether you're working on ideas solo or in a collaborative situation (such as a workshop). If you have sketches, you might as well pick up Marvel, snap some pictures, and stitch them together to create a prototype.

At a certain point your prototype may grow and you'll probably find yourself wanting a higher-fidelity version, whether that's in terms of visual quality, depth/breadth, or presentation of interaction. At that point, you could move on to use Marvel in other ways with other design resources and a more involved workflow, or indeed some of the other prototyping tools and techniques.

Marvel Summary

Product name: Marvel
By: Marvel
Platform: iOS and Android, desktop/laptop web app.
Single user license cost: free version for two projects; $12/month Pro; variable pricing for multiple-user company license.
URL: https://marvelapp.com/

Pros:

- simple, quick, and easy to take sketches and turn them into clickable prototypes
- ideal for testing quick ideas, especially in collaborative working situations

Cons:

- with the iOS/Android app, you're restricted to working in a range of mobile device screen sizes and aspect ratios
- no support for adaptive/responsive designs
- with the iOS/Android app on devices, the limited workflow for supporting larger prototypes and higher-fidelity quickly becomes inefficient and

restrictive. At this point, consider moving to Marvel on desktop/laptop or other tools

Comparable tools:

- Other tools offer support for stitching together flat images to create a prototype with more features, flexibility, and higher fidelity (for example, PDFs/Acrobat, InVision), and these are discussed in this chapter. But there's nothing else of which we're aware with the same basic on-device image capture, prototype creation, and prototype running functionality as Marvel.
- For the laptop/desktop version of Marvel, its feature set closely matches InVision (discussed in more detail in this chapter).

Clickable PDFs

PDF is a file format we all know and love (perhaps the second point is debatable). It's certainly a widely used one, with benefits including the ability to publish and read across different platforms, and generally sensible file sizes (as long as you're careful with the export settings). PDF reading software is widely and freely available, and is installed by default on many platforms and devices. Almost anyone can open a PDF document, so designs are often shared using them with project team members and stakeholders.

The PDF standard includes the ability to create hyperlinks in documents. This means we can create a basic prototype if we're working with a tool that either:

- supports creating links between pages and can export to PDF; examples include Adobe InDesign and Balsamiq (which we talk about in more detail in Chapter 6).
- can edit an existing PDF; examples include Adobe Acrobat Pro and pdfforge

Linking between Pages in a Design Tool

You may already be working in a tool that exports PDFs and is able to group layouts into pages, or an item that can be mapped to a page (such as a canvas or an artboard). If so, you should investigate whether you can go one step further and create internal links between these pages or layout groups.

For example, Adobe InDesign lets you add various kinds of hyperlinks to text or graphical elements. The one we're interested in is the ability to create a hyperlink to a page, as shown below.

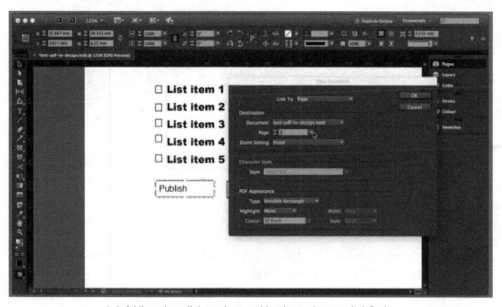

5-2. Adding a hyperlink to a button object in another page in InDesign

Similarly, links created between mockups in Balsamiq will be exported so that they link between mockups on different pages of a PDF.

Editing an Existing PDF to Add Hyperlinks

If you have an existing PDF that presents layouts or mockups for a design you're working on, or if the tool(s) in which you're working can output a PDF but lack the facility to create hyperlinks, you can still use an additional third-party tool to add hyperlinks to pages in your PDF. A tool you may already have access to is Adobe Acrobat Pro, which is a full-featured PDF creation/editing tool, shown below.

5-3. Adding an invisible hyperlink to another page in Adobe Acrobat Pro

Clickable PDFs Summary

Pros:

- easy and cheap creation of basic clickable prototypes if you're already working in tools that can create a PDF
- able to create prototypes across a range of fidelities from sketches, through wireframes, up to high-fidelity mockups
- PDF is a commonly used format so it's well supported across platforms and easy to present and share with your project team, stakeholders, and user research participants
- the ability to present and use prototypes on touch and narrow viewport devices

Cons:

- workflow can be awkward and time-consuming, particularly if you're not already exporting and creating PDFs
- responsive/adaptive presentation of prototypes is limited to an individual PDF's ability to scale
- limited to the very basic functionality that hyperlinks between pages in PDFs supports

Apps that support adding hyperlinks to PDFs include:

- Adobe Acrobat Pro: https://acrobat.adobe.com/uk/en/acrobat/acrobat-pro.html (Windows and Mac)
- Foxit PhantomPDF: https://www.foxitsoftware.com/ (Windows only)
- iSkysoft PDF Editor: https://www.iskysoft.com (Windows and Mac)
- PDFescape: https://www.pdfescape.com/ (web app, use in browser)
- pdfforge PDF Architect Standard: http://www.pdfforge.org/ (Windows and Mac)

Tools Dedicated to Creating Clickable Prototypes

A number of tools have emerged over the past couple of years that have developed the idea of stitching together images to create clickable prototypes. These tools operate on the same principles as the clickable PDF techniques previously described. But since they are tools developed specifically for prototyping, they have features and workflows that make the process of creating, updating, and maintaining a prototype much easier. And most support the processes of sharing, demonstrating, and testing prototypes with integration with other apps and services. All of this adds up to a prototyping workflow that's quicker and easier to get going and maintain.

The typical features these tools offer include:

- bulk upload of multiple images that represent the screens in the prototype
- uploading Sketch or Photoshop files that contain designs for multiple screens and unpacking them to create screens in the prototype
- directly uploading files from file-sharing services such as Dropbox and Google Drive
- syncing between image and/or design files linked through a file-sharing service so that changes to these files will be reflected in the prototype
- workflow to help with the organization of large numbers of screen images into groups or folders
- an edit mode for screens that allows the creation of clickable hotspots to link to other screens
- a selection of transition effects between screens to make prototypes more realistic (particularly those presenting mobile sites or apps)
- a range of interactions that can be acted on beyond simple single-click / tap; such as double-click / tap, swiping, and pinching

- a preview mode that enables you to test your prototype and demo it face-to-face with team members, stakeholders, and user research participants
- features to share a prototype with others via links that open the prototype in a browser
- commenting features so that people reviewing the prototype can leave general feedback or annotations on specific elements

Sketch

Sketch[1] isn't strictly a prototyping tool in its own right, but many of the tools and workflows that we discuss in this chapter are designed to have close integration with Sketch. If you're unfamiliar with Sketch as a design tool, it's worth taking the time to explore and trial. Its vector-based workflow is well-suited to the rapid creation of design wireframes and mockups, and hence to the creation of prototypes.

Unfortunately, it's Mac-only and its creators, Bohemian, indicate that there will be no support on other platforms. Tools such as InVision typically offer integration with Photoshop, so that could be your best option if you're a Windows user.

We'll now take a quick walk-through of InVision (a popular example in this category of tools) to create a prototype from a set of wireframes. This basic workflow represents the kind of steps you'd go through to create a prototype from a set of images using this category of prototyping tool.

We start with a Sketch file containing wireframes for three screens in three separate artboards. The Sketch file is dragged into InVision to create a new project.

The InVision Craft Plugin for Sketch

InVision has developed a plugin for Sketch called Craft[2], which has a number of features that make the workflow for creating and sharing a prototype easier and more powerful. We discuss Craft in some more detail in Appendix A.

---

[1] If you're interested in learning more about Sketch, check out the SitePoint book, *Jump Start Sketch*: https://www.sitepoint.com/premium/books/jump-start-sketch

[2] https://www.invisionapp.com/craft

Because we've given the artboards for each screen sensible names, InVision
understands these and presents the three screens on the *Screens* tab for the
prototype, seen below. As a prototype grows in size and includes more screens,
we can reorder the screens in this listing and arrange them into logical groups to
make our workflow easier.

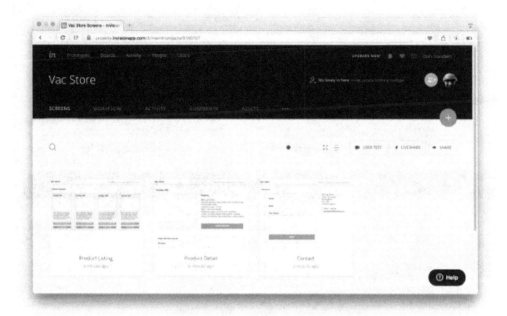

5-4. The *Screens* tab presents the screens in our prototype

When we open up an individual screen for editing, the toolbar at the bottom
allows us to switch between *Preview*, *Build*, *Comment*, and *History* modes.
Selecting *Build* mode gives us a tool for adding a hotspot to the screen as
presented below, which we can then link to other screens.

5-5. Adding hotspots to a screen in *Build* mode so as to link it to other screens (1)

5-6. Adding hotspots to a screen in *Build* mode so as to link it to other screens (2)

You can also note the *Hotspot Template* feature in the figure above, which makes it easier to add the same links to our masthead navigation that is common to all screens. Once we've added hotspots to all our screens, we can then switch to *Preview* mode and click around our prototype to move between screens. And we've created our prototype.

Further features of InVision allow us to work collaboratively on projects; track our workflow (screens can be tagged as *In Progress*, *Needs Review*, *Approved*, and so on); add comments to screens; and share projects with others (regardless of whether or not they're registered InVision users) for demo, feedback, and testing with users.

InVision's ability to accept Sketch files and Photoshop files makes for a rapid workflow if you use these tools to create wireframes or mockups. But InVision and other similar tools (such as Marvel and Concept.ly) can also import images. All this means is that the fidelity of prototypes that we create using these kind of tools is dictated only by the fidelity of the input files and screens therein. So we can use these tools to create prototypes from sketches, wireframes, higher-fidelity mockups—all the way up to full fidelity design comps.

5-7. Importing a high-fidelity comp that was created in Photoshop into InVision to create a prototype

InVision Summary

By: InVision
Platform: Desktop web browser interface.
Single-user license cost: free version for one prototype; $15/month for three prototypes; $25/month for unlimited prototypes; $99/month for unlimited prototypes for up to five team members.
URL: http://www.invisionapp.com

Pros:

- flexibility to create prototypes with images of any level of fidelity
- quick and easy to create a basic prototype from your existing designs, with lots of features to support workflow; collaboration; design feedback; and demoing, sharing, and testing
- easily create multiscreened prototypes by importing Sketch and Photoshop files with screens defined by artboards or layers/layer groups
- integration with file-sharing services such as Dropbox means that changes to your designs can be automatically transferred into your prototype
- free to get going and trial with one full-scale fully featured prototype
- integrates well with existing design tools and workflows; for example, using Sketch or Photoshop to create wireframes or mockups
- the Craft plugin for Sketch created by InVision brings a solid set of features to Sketch to make prototyping with these tools quicker and more powerful (we discuss Craft in more detail in Appendix A)

Cons:

- you're forced to work with a range of mobile device screen sizes and aspect ratios
- there's no support for adaptive/responsive designs, so each prototype is fixed to a defined screen size / aspect ratio
- with InVision, there are no built-in drawing tools so you'll have to use other tools to create designs; other tools in this category (such as Marvel and UXPin) support images and/or drawing

Comparable tools:

- Marvel: https://marvelapp.com
- UXPin: https://www.uxpin.com
- Concept.ly: http://concept.ly

Links to other tools mentioned:

- Dropbox: https://www.dropbox.com
- Sketch: https://www.sketchapp.com
- Photoshop: http://www.adobe.com/products/photoshop.html

Summary

In this chapter, we looked at tools that help us to create an interactive prototype using outputs from existing design workflow processes. Those outputs could be hand-drawn sketches, wireframes, or higher-fidelity mockups produced using tools such as Balsamiq, Sketch, or Photoshop.

We explored the Marvel mobile app, which bridges the gap between paper prototyping and interactive prototypes brilliantly, particularly when you're working on ideas and sketches collaboratively.

We looked at creating PDF interactive prototypes, either using tools that can output a clickable PDF (such as InDesign or Balsamiq) or tools for editing PDFs (such as Adobe Acrobat Pro or Foxit PhantomPDF).

Finally, we covered a new generation of dedicated prototyping tools (such as InVision) that add features and workflows, making the job of creating interactive prototypes from existing designs easier, more collaborative, and powerful.

In the next chapter, we discuss various tools containing drawing/editing functionality, so they are seen as a more all-in-one option for creating prototypes.

Chapter **6**

Integrated Tools for Drawing and Creating Prototypes

Where Chapter 5 looked at tools aimed at creating a prototype from a set of existing images, this chapter looks at tools that also provide some kind of drawing and design capability.

In the previous chapter, we were using other tools to create designs (such as paper sketches, Photoshop, or Sketch); the tools in this chapter offer a more integrated solution. You'll probably find there are advantages and disadvantages to both approaches here. The clear advantage is that you only have to learn and use one single tool to create your prototypes. The corresponding disadvantage is that there's a lack of flexibility and you're locked into the design capabilities of that tool. This lack of flexibility may feel more significant where you (or your team) are already using other tools to create designs of some form.

As with the tools in the other chapters, we suggest you read through and perhaps try some of them out for yourself, in order to get a feel for what will work best for you and your team.

Common Features in this Category of Prototyping Tools

Drawing and Design Features

Most of the tools we talk about here share a set of drawing and design features that make the creation of prototypes easier and quicker. Typically, these features help irrespective of your level of design skill or familiarity with design tools. Thinking about what you'll be designing as you build a prototype should help you to understand the benefits of features such as:

- Being able to configure grids to help position elements.
- Visual hinting of element size and position, and tools for controlling the distribution of multiple selected elements, making it simple to create, size, and position elements in a consistent and visually coherent way.
- The ability to easily constrain shape elements as you create them; for example, constraining an ellipse to a sphere.
- A library of example design templates (for example, layouts for different device sizes and aspect ratios) and symbols (such as form fields or iOS/Android native UI elements), and the ability to create your own symbols for elements that are common and consistent throughout a design.

Features Galore

It's worth noting that many of the drawing features discussed here are found in other standalone design tools (such as Sketch or Photoshop), which you might use alongside the tools discussed in Chapter 5.

Increased Support for Prototyping Interactivity

The tools we've looked at so far have been generally limited to creating hotspots to trigger transitioning between screens. In this category, the tools support the creation of prototypes with more powerful and flexible interactivity, such as:

- The ability to show/hide elements based on user interaction.
- Different temporary or persistent states of elements, screens, or the overall app; for example, you might want to display different elements and templates for signed-in users compared to those not signed in.
- The ability to accept user input and present different elements/templates based upon that input. This would allow stronger prototyping of a search function and different results displayed for different searches, for example.

Prototyping Workflow Features

Much like the newer tools described in Chapter 5, some of the tools discussed in this chapter include features that help with your prototyping workflow, such as:

- The ability to set and track the status of a design unit (such as a template or an element) in your workflow.
- Support for collaborative working by teams to share and distribute the work of creating a prototype.
- Annotation and commenting features so that you can capture and act upon feedback on your designs.
- The ability to publish and distribute a prototype for sharing with the project team, stakeholders, and user research participants for testing.

Let's leap in and start exploring some of the tools in this category.

Balsamiq

Balsamiq is a tool that has been around for a while now and many people will be familiar with having used it to create wireframes. It has a deservedly good reputation as being easy with which to get going. Folks creating their first wireframes can come to grips with its drag-and-drop interface very easily, even if they have little significant experience of design and other design tools.

Balsamiq Mockups is a desktop application for both Windows and Mac. There's also a web version called myBalsamiq and other plugin versions (such as one that sits on top of Google Drive for collaborative working). From hereon, we'll just refer to Balsamiq's desktop version. We advise investigating the various options—the differences between them and their pricing models—if it seems as if Balsamiq could be a useful tool for you.

We're interested in Balsamiq because beyond basic wireframing it offers us the ability to create interactive prototypes. Most elements on a design can be turned into links, and those links can link to other pages/screens (Balsamiq calls these **mockups**) in a project, as demonstrated below. That's enough functionality to create basic clickable prototypes.

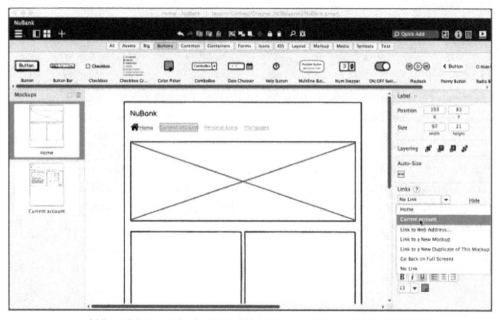

6-1. Adding a link to a navigation item to link between mockups in a Balsamiq prototype

Balsamiq has two **skins** (you could think of these as being akin to themes) with which you can present your designs: Sketch and Wireframe. There's actually little difference between the two, with both options using a Comic-Sans-like font (although it's not actually Comic Sans). The Sketch theme lives up to its name and presents designs with a distinctly hand-drawn feel. Some designers dislike Balsamiq because they feel it makes their work look ugly. Others like it for its designs being presented sketch-like with a lo-fi feel. This helps convey their work-in-progress nature and encourages open and honest feedback around layout and functionality, rather than design aesthetics. If you dislike sketching by hand—or think you're simply bad at it—Balsamiq may be a good tool for you to explore and present early-stage prototype designs.

Balsamiq features minimal sophisticated design tools, instead focusing on a simple drag-and-drop interface with a wide selection of predrawn, fully scalable symbols. These include common user interface elements such as form fields, navigation menus, tabs, buttons, and a range of icons, as displayed below.. This reliance on a library of symbols means it may not be so useful when you need to design with original, non-standard UI elements. That said, you can bring in your own images to use as assets (the easiest way is to drag-and-drop) and create custom symbols to use across pages/screens in a prototype by grouping elements together

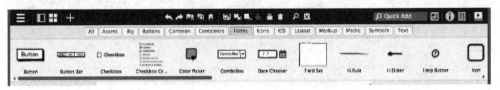

6-2. Balsamiq includes a wide variety of predrawn symbols that you drag-and-drop onto page/screen to create a design

Positioning elements on the canvas for a page/screen in Balsamiq is straightforward with a grid, as shown below. Automatic alignment guides appear as you place and move items, and there are features for aligning, sizing, and distributing multiple selected elements.

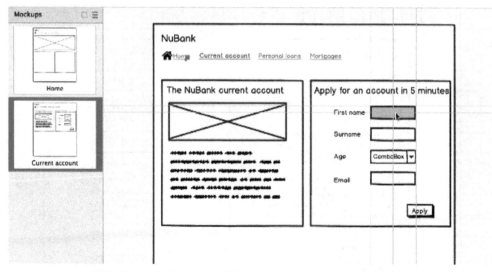

6-3. Alignment guides help quickly position elements relative to each other

When you're ready to demo your prototype and share it with your project team and others for testing, Balsamiq offers several of options:

Full-screen presentation mode   This removes all the Balsamiq user interface (there is some minimal interface for controlling settings of the presentation mode that can be hidden) to display your clickable prototype. See figure 6-4 below.

Export to PDF   The links in your prototype will be maintained as links in the PDF so that viewers can click around your prototype. The scalable nature of Balsamiq and the images in a PDF mean that you can share and test your prototype on mobile and tablet devices.

Web-based option   myBalsamiq allows you to share your prototype with others with which to view, interact, and collaborate.

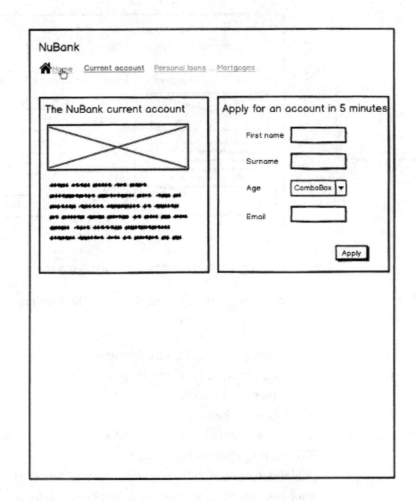

6-4. Balsamiq's full-screen presentation mode is ideal for presenting and testing a prototype. The toolbar and settings for this mode have been hidden.

Balsamiq Summary

Product name: Balsamiq Mockups
By: Balsamiq
Platform: Mac, Windows, and a web-based version called myBalsamiq.
Single-user license cost: $89
URL: https://balsamiq.com/

Pros:

- easy to learn and use, even for those with limited experience of other design tools
- a comprehensive library of predrawn symbols and good design layout tools makes it quick and easy to design a variety of common layouts using the simple drag-and-drop interface
- simple linking functionality enables straightforward and rapid creation of basic clickable prototypes from wireframe-style layout designs
- low-fidelity, sketch-like presentation helps to create prototypes that are clearly a work-in-progress, encouraging useful feedback
- the custom symbols feature helps to reduce duplicated effort and complexity when linking together large numbers of pages/screens with common elements such as navigation
- the full-screen presentation mode makes it straightforward to run an observed user test
- able to create a clickable PDF of your prototype for sharing and remote user testing

Cons:

- the wireframe/sketch style and lack of flexible design/drawing tools limits designers to creating basic low-fidelity prototypes (which all have that distinctive Balsamiq style and feel)
- unlikely to be the most efficient tool with which to create a large prototype from scratch
- no concept of information architecture / site hierarchy, so prototyping and testing a full site structure will take time, and potentially be inefficient and error-prone
- no way to prototype UI transitions and animation
- a lack of responsive/adaptive presentation—you'll be able to share a PDF that will display on different devices at different widths, but it won't be a truly responsive prototype
- working collaboratively on a project could be tricky and risky, since you'd be working with a single Balsamiq project file; that said, the web application and plugin versions of Balsamiq offer collaborative working features, and may be a better option if you're likely to need them

Comparable tools:

- Mockingbird: https://gomockingbird.com/
- Pencil Project: http://pencil.evolus.vn/

OmniGraffle

OmniGraffle is a high-quality diagramming and illustration tool. There are versions for macOS and iOS, but we'll be referring to the desktop version here. There's plenty of crossover between the desktop and iOS versions but also some differences, so make sure you review these if you're considering using OmniGraffle.

Designers can use OmniGraffle for a range of purposes. At fffunction, we use it a lot for producing information architecture (for example, sitemaps) and flow and mapping deliverables (such as user task model diagrams). We'll discuss it here because it can also be used to develop wireframe-style layouts that can be linked together to create a clickable prototype.

OmniGraffle differs from Balsamiq in the quality of design presentation. It produces layout designs of higher quality than Balsamiq, yet still obviously wireframe in style, as can be seen in figure 6-5. As with Balsamiq much of its strength lies in its easy-to-use drawing interface; this makes it easy to create elements on a canvas, then use the sizing, spacing, and alignment guides to lay them out. There are plenty of workflow tools to help you organize elements on a canvas as you create a large number of templates, screens, or wireframes. There is an established market for **stencils**, which are libraries of ready-made templates and elements to include in wireframes and prototypes. This includes OmniGroup's Stenciltown[1] and the popular Graffletopia[2].

[1.] https://stenciltown.omnigroup.com
[2.] https://www.graffletopia.com/

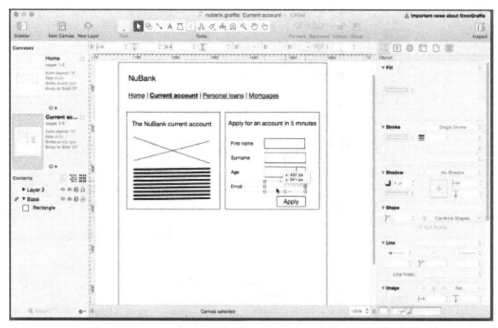

6-5. OmniGraffle has similar features to Balsamiq, making layout design a breeze; however, the quality of the designs produced by OmniGraffle is noticeably better.

OmniGraffle features a solid set of drawing/design tools, such as a pen tool that allows you to draw custom shapes using Bézier handles. Its design workflow features (such as layer and element group organization and control) and element inspector/control features (control over an element's stroke, fill, and drop shadow)—evident in the figure below—will be familiar to designers who have used other design tools such as Photoshop.

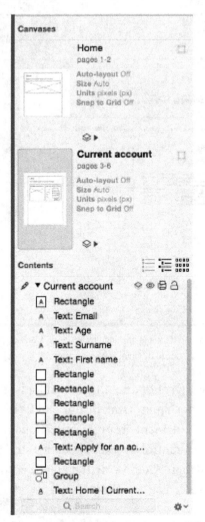

6-6. OmniGraffle's canvas, layout, group, and elements organization features will be familiar to designers used to the powerful controls offered by other design tools

OmniGraffle's ability to create prototypes is made possible by one particular feature: the Action property on elements. Unfortunately this feature is only available in OmniGraffle Pro, which means an extra cost for the license.

There are several actions available upon clicking an element. The ones we're interested in are the ability to jump to another canvas (*Jumps Elsewhere*), and to toggle the display of layers (*Shows or Hides Layers*). Using these actions you can add links and controls to a prototype to move between canvases representing screens/pages and add interactivity by showing and hiding elements on a canvas.

Further power and flexibility that could aid advanced users comes with the ability to add actions, which runs some AppleScript.

 AppleScript

It's beyond the scope of this book to explain **AppleScript**. In simple terms it's an automation scripting language available in macOS that allows the control of applications supporting it. Since OmniGraffle does support it, you can use AppleScript to manipulate layers, and objects within them. There's a helpful Fuzzy Math blog post[3] describes a technique that uses AppleScript to show/hide a layer of annotation notes on a prototype.

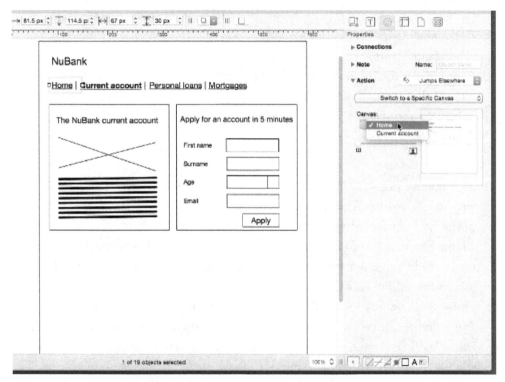

6-7. Adding an action to an element to jump to a canvas when clicked.

Prototypes built with OmniGraffle can be presented, shared, and distributed in a variety of ways. OmniGraffle Pro includes a Presentation mode, which is intended for live presentation of diagrams/images (similar to the Full-screen

---

[3.] http://blog.fuzzymath.com/2010/02/24/prototyping-with-omnigraffle-showhide-annotations/

presentation mode offered by Balsamiq). We can use this to present a prototype to collaborators, or to users for testing.

Other export methods include PDF and an HTML image map. Both of these options offer the ability to share and distribute your prototype to remote collaborators and users. As with Balsamiq, exporting to PDF potentially allows pseudo-responsive presentation of a prototype: the PDF will scale on different width screens. But there's no true responsive or adaptive support in prototypes created in OmniGraffle.

OmniGraffle Summary

Product name: OmniGraffle Pro for Mac
By: The Omni Group
Platform: Mac only, there is also a version for iOS.
Single-user license cost: $199.99
URL: https://www.omnigroup.com/omnigraffle/

Pros:

- high-quality presentation wireframes and prototypes
- easy to use, yet has flexible and powerful layout tools
- prototypes are easy to create with basic actions on elements
- a large community of OmniGraffle stencil providers makes it simple to find ready-made templates and elements to include in your prototypes, while a mix of free and chargeable libraries are available
- prototypes can be presented, distributed, and shared in several ways
- AppleScript can be used to add custom functionality (with caveats, see Cons)
- OmniGraffle is a good tool for producing other design deliverables such as sitemaps and user flow diagrams

Cons:

- Mac (and iPad) only
- far from being the cheapest option and you'll need OmniGraffle Pro to build prototypes

- AppleScript can only provide functionality up to a point and it's not particularly easy to learn and work with, particularly if you have no or limited coding/scripting experience
- limited to wireframe-style fidelity
- no ability to prototype UI transitions and animation
- no responsive/adaptive presentation: you can share a PDF that will display on different devices at different widths, but you can't create a truly responsive prototype

Comparable tools:

- Axure (discussed shortly)
- There are other tools offering comparable diagramming functionality to OmniGraffle, but these are irrelevant to the creation of interactive prototypes

Axure

Axure's full name is Axure RP, with RP standing for Rapid Prototyping. Designers (particularly those working in UX) have been using Axure for creating diagrams, wireframes, and prototypes for a number of years. It's an incredibly powerful, flexible design tool with lots of features, as evident in figure 6-8. With that power and flexibility comes a sizable price tag and a potentially steep learning curve.

Axure's design tool set combines features that we've already seen in Balsamiq and OmniGraffle, then adds a wealth of extra features with further prototyping power on top. Much like Balsamiq, layout design is achieved primarily through a comprehensive library of premade symbols, elements, and icons. You create an interface by dragging and dropping combinations of these and arranging them on a canvas—all with the help of a sophisticated set of alignment, layout, and sizing guides and tools.

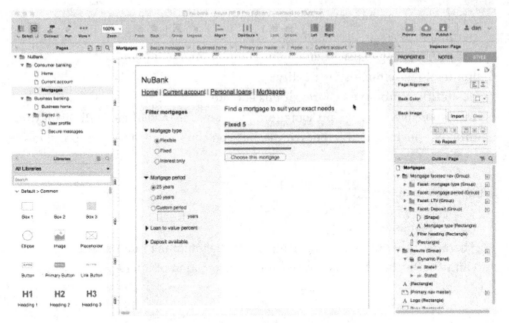

6-8. The Axure workspace

Axure brings features for organizing large prototypes with lots of pages/templates. The Pages panel presents pages in the current project and enables them to be organized into a hierarchical structure, with pages and groups of pages in folders, as depicted below.

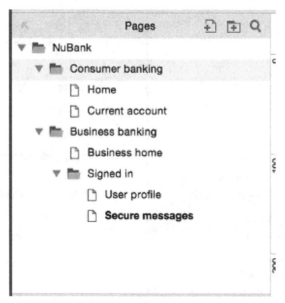

6-9. The *Pages* panel helps you to organize a large prototyping project into a logical hierarchical structure with folders

Axure's power for designing interfaces and interaction comes with each page you create having a hierarchical element model within which all the elements are contained, shown in figure 6-10. When you drop a new element onto a page, it's added to the hierarchy. Then, as you group elements together, the model is updated accordingly and you can name elements or groups of elements.

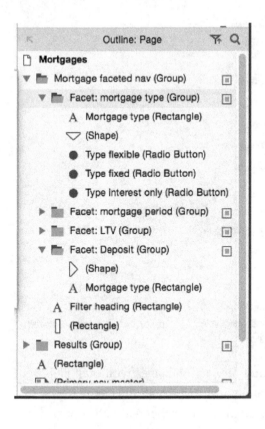

6-10. The *Outline* panel presents the elements on a page in a hierarchical model. Here you can see the elements that make up a faceted navigation

As well as giving you organizational power and control over all the elements in your design, it also brings in Axure's fully featured events model. Each element can have events and event handlers added to it, so you can react to an event with any one of a comprehensive set of actions, going beyond the basic ability to link and jump to other pages, as seen with the other tools covered. With Axure, you can effect changes to other elements in the page—as seen below—or beyond, on other pages.

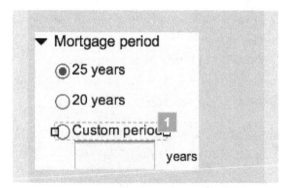

6-11. Setting events on page elements in Axure. Here, events and actions have been added to enable a text field (and focus on it) for a custom value when the custom radio button is selected, and to disable it again when another radio button in the group is selected (1).

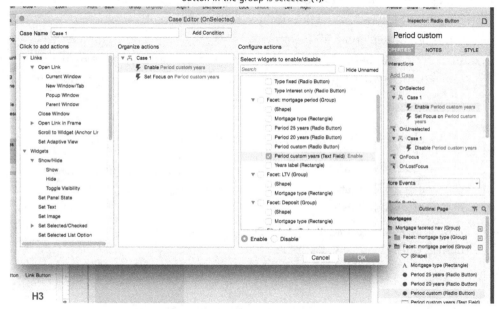

6-12. Setting events on page elements in Axure. Here, events and actions have been added to enable a text field (and focus on it) for a custom value when the custom radio button is selected, and to disable it again when another radio button in the group is selected (2).

Examples of the kinds of interactivity you can implement using Axure's event and actions model in your prototype include:

- showing and hiding elements
- changing text on labels
- enabling and disabling elements

- moving, rotating, or resizing elements, and moving elements forwards or backwards in the view
- logic actions allowing you to implement features such as list sorting or ordering, and setting and getting variable values to implement your own custom interactions

Plus, you can, of course, move between pages, giving us the ability to link together canvases to build multiview prototypes.

Axure is the first tool we've looked at that offers features for creating prototypes that will work across different screen dimensions. They're adaptive rather than responsive (see the note below on this) and they allow you to define different screen dimensions, and have your designs behave differently as you move between those dimensions; for example, you might design a form for a wide desktop screen with fields laid out horizontally as depicted in figure 6-13, but then move them to stack up vertically on a narrow mobile screen as shown in figure 6-14.

The Difference between Adaptive and Responsive

Put simply, in an **adaptive** design, elements will snap into different positions or different dimensions at a number of predefined viewport widths. In a **responsive** design, elements resize smoothly and continuously as viewport width changes.

A more detailed explanation of the differences between responsive and adaptive designs can be found on CSS Tricks.[4]

---

4. https://css-tricks.com/the-difference-between-responsive-and-adaptive-design/

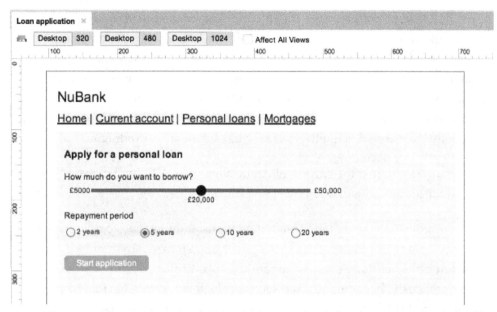

6-13. Using Axure's adaptive views feature to design different layouts for a form for different viewport widths (1)

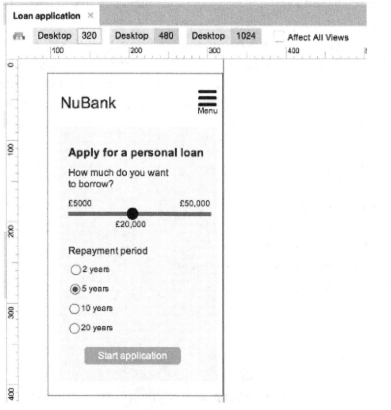

6-14. Using Axure's adaptive views feature to design different layouts for a form for different viewport widths (2)

Axure builds your prototypes as HTML/CSS. This makes it suitable for distributing and sharing your prototypes, although there may be some issues; for instance, you'll need to install an extension to view the HTML version using Chrome. You're also given the option of using some of the code Axure generates as the starting point for your production code. You may want to do this in consultation with a front-end developer if you're not one: the markup produced is generally of reasonable quality, but may be lacking for a production build.

We've barely scratched the surface of Axure's feature set. Other potentially useful features for prototyping include:

- A comprehensive set of notes and annotations allowing you to document the behavior of your prototype and the screens and elements that make it up. This includes the ability to export a functional specification document that comprehensively documents the screens, elements, and behaviors in your prototype, which you can share with designers and developers.
- "Masters" that allow you to share common elements across screens (analogous to symbols in other tools such as Sketch).
- "Dynamic panels" that are used to achieve a variety of tasks including creating multistate elements (such as image carousels); creating draggable elements; and pinning elements in position in the browser viewport (for example, to create a **sticky navigation** that stays at the top of the screen as the user scrolls up and down a page).

Axure Summary

Product name: Axure RP
By: Axure Software Solutions
Platform: Mac and Windows
Single-user license cost: $495 or $29/month
URL: http://www.axure.com/

Pros:

- very robust and flexible
- powerful layout design tools
- user interface and feature set supports building of large, complex prototypes and the workflow and organization involved

- comprehensive events model allows prototyping of all sorts of sites, features, interactions, and functionality
- animation and transitions can be prototyped
- although presentation is fundamentally in a wireframe style, there is some flexibility to increase fidelity for some or all of your prototypes
- comprehensive notes and annotations feature set for communicating your designs with the project team and stakeholders
- creates shareable HTML (with caveats, see Cons)
- adaptive views allow consideration of designing across different device widths (with caveats, see Cons)

Cons:

- steep learning curve
- arguably expensive (with value for money being a factor for consideration)
- shareable HTML is not without problems; for example, viewing in Chrome requires a Chrome Extension to be installed
- adaptive views are tricky to set up, time-consuming, and unable to present true responsive designs
- collaborative working could be tricky and prone to problems, although there are some features in Axure that support it (such as "team projects" and "Axure Share")
- there's an argument that Axure's feature-rich interactive prototypes could be created in HTML/CSS prototypes (see Chapter 7)

Comparable tools:
Justinmind Prototyper: https://www.justinmind.com

Keynote and PowerPoint

We have some fairly high-level specialist design tools in this chapter. At this point, it's important to highlight a category of tools that perhaps one wouldn't immediately think of as design tools, but which are great for prototyping: presentation creation tools Keynote and PowerPoint.

Lets look at why these tools are perfect for prototyping and hence worthy of consideration:

- One of them is usually installed on most computers, and the majority of people know how to use them too—at the very least to view a presentation.
- Consequently, it's typically easy for anyone to create a prototype and share it.
- And because it's already installed, those working in corporations or the public service who have little control over the software purchased can jump ahead and create their prototypes, rather than wait for a specialist tool to be installed.
- The basic drawing and design features offered are similar to those described for useful prototyping tools in this chapter; this includes features such as layout to grid, element alignment guides and tools, easy importing of images and other media, and easy publishing or sharing.
- The typical prototype presentation created with these tools hits the ideal point on the visual fidelity spectrum: not too sketchy or messy, not too polished and production-ready.
- They're super-hot right now! If you need evidence, have a look at the work of Google Ventures and their week-long design sprints—brilliantly documented in their book *Sprint: How to Solve Big Problems and Test New Ideas in Just Five Days*[5]. The tool they favor for prototyping is Keynote (though they grudgingly mention PowerPoint). Of the 100+ design sprints they've run (at the time of writing their book), Keynote has been the preferred prototyping tool.

Using a tool to create prototypes that is intended for creating slides and presenting on a screen comes with a clear drawback worthy of your consideration: it's a fixed viewport with which to work and there's no scrolling. Both Keynote and PowerPoint come with a selection of default presentation slide dimensions and aspect ratios. You can use your own custom dimensions, and as your familiarity with using Keynote/PowerPoint for prototyping grows, you probably will. But changing the presentation dimensions of a prototype can be problematic, with scaling and positioning of elements on slides changing in unpredictable ways. So take some time to consider the presentation aspect ratio and dimensions you'll work in based upon what you're prototyping, and how and where you'll want to share and present your prototype. Given all this, it's worth noting that there's no support for any kind of responsive or adaptive designs in any prototypes created with Keynote or PowerPoint.

[5.] https://www.goodreads.com/book/show/25814544-sprint

Three Approaches for Using Keynote and PowerPoint for Prototyping

Keynote and PowerPoint bring flexibility in their prototyping abilities. You can use them in three different ways (or indeed in some combination of these).

Creating a Clickable Prototype from an Existing Design

You can import existing designs such as sketches, wireframes, and other design mockups and turn them into clickable prototypes. You'd do this by importing images representing screens or templates from your designs into slides, and then adding invisible or opaque hit areas over elements in your designs, and linking these areas to other slides, screens, or templates, as shown below.

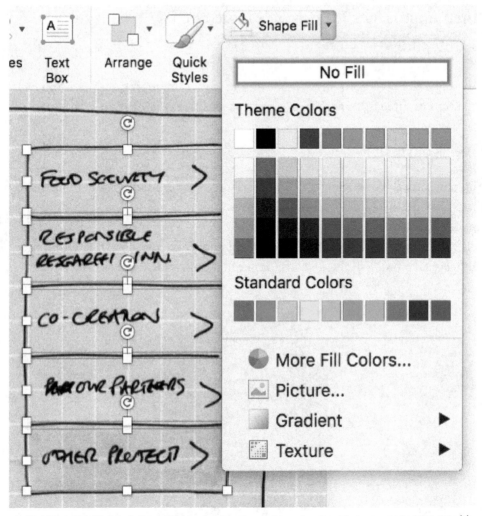

6-15. Adding clickable links in PowerPoint by drawing opaque shapes over items in a menu and adding links (1)

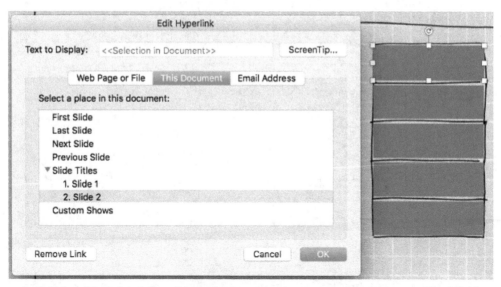

6-16. Adding clickable links in PowerPoint by drawing opaque shapes over items in a menu and adding links (2)

Using Keynote and PowerPoint in this way is comparable to the workflow we described for tools such as Marvel in <u>Chapter 5</u>.

Using the Built-in Design Tools to Create a Prototype

You can use the design and drawing tools for creating and laying out screens or templates and their user interfaces and elements. Basic shape tools, layout and alignment features, and element properties such as fonts and colors should provide all you need to design and present most layouts and user interfaces as prototypes, as seen below.

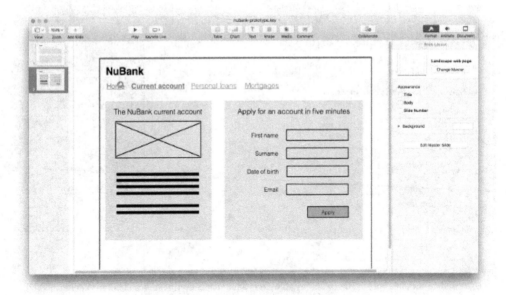

6-17. Prototyping simple web page layouts in Keynote

If you want to go further, some specialist symbol libraries offer the ability to incorporate ready-made layouts and user interface elements. The best known of these is Keynotopia[6], which offers a comprehensive range of template bundles for both Keynote and PowerPoint, along with useful guides and resources to help you come to grips with creating prototypes using Keynote and Powerpoint.

Prototyping Animations

You can use the tools' features to add animation to presentations, and design user interface transitions and animations in your prototypes.

We've deliberately avoided going into much depth around prototyping animations throughout the book (we mention some tools—such as Framer—that are ideally suited to prototyping animation in Appendix A) and we'll avoid going into great depth on using Keynote and PowerPoint for this here. But it's certainly worth noting that these tools offer the option (again, let's remind ourselves they're just Office Suite tools for creating presentations!).

---

6. http://keynotopia.com/

In both PowerPoint and Keynote, you have the ability to move objects along paths and change their opacity. These two basic animation techniques are the most useful for prototyping.

There's also an easy way to do advanced animations using a slide transition: it automatically works out the transition and animation between the same objects on two slides. You set up a start slide and an end slide, and the transition automatically creates the animation between the two slides. In Keynote, this transition is called Magic Move (depicted below), and in PowerPoint it's called Morph.

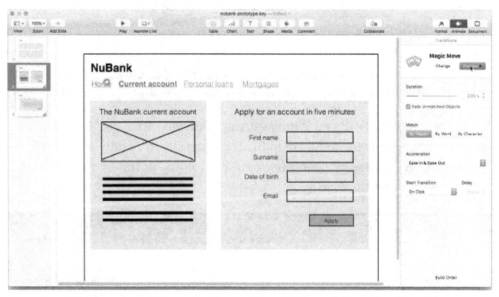

6-18. Prototyping a simple user interface transition using Keynote's Magic Move feature (1)

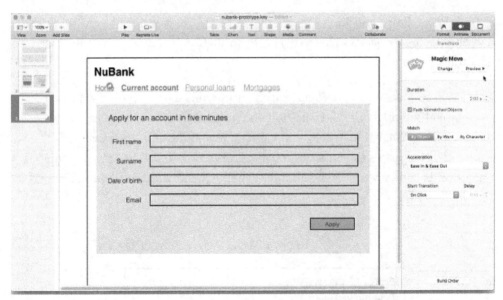

6-19. Prototyping a simple user interface transition using Keynote's Magic Move feature (2)

In PowerPoint (specifically on Windows), the *Animation Pane* enables you to order and manipulate the timing of individual elements in an animation, seen below. This level of fine-grained control makes prototyping more complex user interface animations possible.

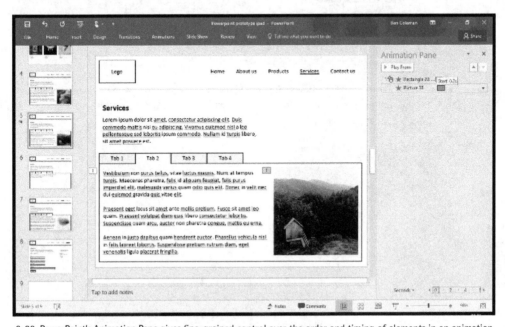

6-20. PowerPoint's Animation Pane gives fine-grained control over the order and timing of elements in an animation

Remember that while animations can add an extra dimension to your prototypes, they should be used judiciously. Avoid using them just because you can—and absolutely no "confetti" or "sparkle" transitions, please! We'd argue that the same caution should be applied to using animations in presentations (although that's possibly overstepping our remit here).

If you're looking to prototype specific user interface interactions in depth, you should certainly consider trying these tools before coming to grips with anything else that may be more involved and complex.

Sharing Prototypes Created in Keynote and Powerpoint

If team members and stakeholders have the same presentation app as you, you can share the Keynote or PowerPoint file with them. We've already mentioned this as an obvious benefit to using these tools. There are also options for when you want to share your prototype file with folk without the relevant app installed. PowerPoint has a feature to save a presentation as a "PowerPoint Show," which is standalone and autoplays (which can also help with font incompatibility problems that sometimes crop up when sharing a presentation between computers and devices).

Both Keynote and Powerpoint offer support for running presentations (and hence your prototypes) on smartphone and tablet devices through native applications that are available across most devices and platforms. Compatibility and costs vary: Keynote is only available on compatible iOS devices where it's free. Powerpoint, by contrast, is available across iOS and Android devices and is free to open and display a presentation, but you'll need an Office 365 subscription if you want to edit a presentation on a device. You can share files with these apps on devices through email, or through integrations with relevant services including Dropbox, iCloud, and OneDrive.

You could also consider exporting your prototype as a PDF. Both Keynote and Powerpoint offer this option, and links created between slides and screens in your presentation will be honored as clickable links between pages and screens in the PDF.

Keynote also offers the option to export a presentation as HTML. The export uses **Scalable Vector Graphics (SVG)**, which means that the presentation is able to adapt to varying screen sizes, so you can potentially share and present your prototype on different devices.

Whether you're exporting as PDF or HTML, or running your prototype in presentation mode, you should set the presentation to react only to hyperlinks, and not mouse clicks (this is what you'd generally want a presentation to do, and definitely not your prototype). In Keynote, this is achieved by switching the *Presentation Type* in the Document properties inspector from *Normal* to *Links Only*. For PowerPoint, select all your slides and then hit the transition tab. Make sure the checkbox for *on mouse click* is unchecked to ensure your presentation will not advance on any click.

If you're using these tools to prototype animations, you may want to explore the options offered for exporting a presentation to video formats such as QuickTime or MP4. There are various options available on Keynote and Powerpoint across Mac and Windows platforms (since they're hardware/software-dependent) for saving a self-advancing or presenter-controlled slideshow.

Keynote & Powerpoint Summary

Keynote

Product name: Keynote
By: Apple
Platform: Mac, iOS
Single-user license cost: free on compatible Mac and iOS devices and operating systems
URL: http://www.apple.com/keynote/

PowerPoint

Product name: PowerPoint
By: Microsoft
Platform: Windows, Mac, iOS, Android
Single-user license cost: $109.99 desktop (also available with the Microsoft Office Suite and various bundles/subscriptions); free for mobile (but you'll need an Office Suite subscription to edit a presentation on a device)
URL: https://products.office.com/en-gb/powerpoint

Pros:

- most people have used Keynote or PowerPoint at least once, and this familiarity means that there's little to no learning curve, lowering the barrier to entry for creating prototypes
- it's likely you, your team, and your stakeholders already have access to these tools; as a result, there are fewer cost and installation considerations, and sharing and collaborating on prototypes is straightforward
- there's a good range of options for easy sharing and presentation of your prototype amongst team members and stakeholders, as well as for user research
- you can prototype user interface animations
- you can prototype a range of fidelities: from making sketches clickable; through using the design tools to create midlevel, wireframe-style prototypes; up to using libraries such as Keynotopia to create higher-fidelity prototypes

Cons:

- you're limited to a single-size fixed viewport and there's no scrolling available; it can also be tricky changing viewport/aspect ratio mid-design
- there's no support for responsive or adaptive designs in your prototypes
- as like other tools (such as Balsamiq), there's no concept of information architecture or site hierarchy; as a result, prototyping and testing a full site structure will take some time, and can quickly become inefficient and error-prone
- there's no easy way to share common elements (for example, a site navigation bar) across multiple screens in a way that they can be updated in one place
- collaborative design can be problematic where multiple team members are editing the same set of files; however, both Keynote and PowerPoint staff have been working on features to support collaborative working on presentations, which should help make collaborative prototyping easier too

Adobe XD

Adobe have been working on a new application for quite some time; specifically, to aid designers working on website and apps design. This app reportedly aims to replace Adobe Fireworks, a tool that's been in use for many years for UI design, but which is now dormant. At the time of writing, the new tool is still in beta (although it may well have come out of beta by the time the book is published), and has been through a number of iterations in various guises. It's currently called Adobe Experience Design, or Adobe XD.

The aim of Adobe XD is broader than other tools we've discussed so far because it spans the prototype fidelity range right up to full fidelity. This means it can potentially be used to design all the way through to the delivery of production build assets. That aspect is beyond the scope of this book, but it's certainly one to watch; and there's still an option for us to use XD to create prototypes today.

As with most tools in this chapter, the design and drawing tool set includes useful features many designers will be familiar with, including:

- artboards, layers, and element group workflow, which help with the organization of large design projects and the units within them, such as pages or templates down to individual elements
- tools to help with rapid layout design including grids; alignment and spacing hints; and distribution of groups of selected elements
- creation of reusable symbols from groups of elements, as well as a symbol library to organize them (although, at the time of writing, there are some notable restrictions with symbols compared to other prototyping tools)

In addition, there are many features that are of interest to us for creating and sharing interactive prototypes, including:

- A *Prototype* view: enables the creation of links between artboards for templates and pages in designs, and the visualization and organization of these links.
- An online prototype-sharing option: automatically publishes a design to the cloud for easy sharing with project participants. Once published, prototypes can be shared with others via a link, and those reviewing the prototype can comment on it.
- Real-time device preview: by installing an Android or iOS app on a mobile device and then connecting it to a desktop or laptop running Adobe XD with a USB cable, you can preview changes you make to your designs on the device in real time.

Repeat grid (depicted below): a powerful feature that takes a design for an element such as a **teaser block** (a teaser to an article with an image, heading, abstract, and link to the full article) and repeats it across a horizontal or vertical grid. Once repeated, styles for elements can be changed globally across the repeat grid; content can be varied across the items within the grid; and images can be dropped into the grid and applied across the elements within it.

6-21. The powerful Repeat Grid feature allows you to take a design for an element, repeat that design across a grid, then vary content across the grid. Designs for element grids can be created with realistic content very quickly.

It's worth noting that although these features are potentially useful for creating prototypes, they're not without their problems and restrictions while Adobe XD is in beta. For example, the *Prototype* view that visualizes links between pages and templates in a prototype can very quickly become unwieldy and hard to interpret, even for a simple prototype with just a few pages, as you can see below. And there's currently a notable absence of features for creating responsive or adaptive prototypes.

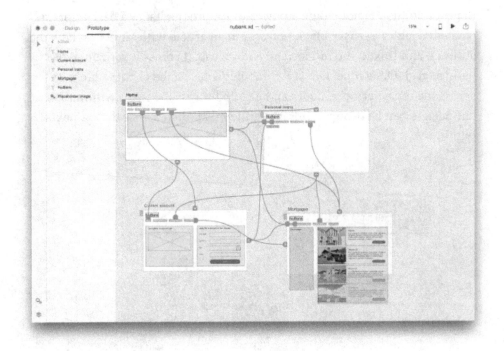

6-22. It's hard to visualize links between even a small number of templates in the *Prototype* view

Right now, Adobe XD displays promise as being a very powerful tool for creating prototypes, and beyond that for creating designs and assets ready for app and website production builds. Adobe's beta program for the app is demonstrably user-centered with a democratic feature request and development program, and a team who are obviously paying attention to user feedback. But there are problems with the various features, and the product is yet to live up to its full promise. As it matures and moves out of beta we'd expect these problems to be resolved, and Adobe XD becoming a handy tool for designing and prototyping websites and apps.

If you've bought into the Adobe ecosystem (for example, you're a Creative Cloud subscriber), you probably already have access to Adobe XD. It's worth experimenting with to see if it can help you create useful interactive prototypes.

Adobe XD Summary

Product name: Adobe Experience Design (XD)
By: Adobe

Platform: Mac and Windows.

Single-user license cost: currently available for free download as it is in beta. Release cost is unknown.

URL: http://www.adobe.com/products/experience-design.html

Pros:

- as it's been designed and built specifically for designing websites and apps, its feature set and workflow are ideally suited to the creation of interactive prototypes
- it's well-suited to the design of prototypes through a range of fidelities, right up to a production-ready fidelity
- easy sharing of prototypes is built into the core product and works well
- the interface, tool set, and workflow will be familiar to users of Adobe tools, but have all been thoughtfully included and designed to suit the needs of website and app design
- as a beta, it's currently freely available for anyone to download and try
- the beta program is notably user-centered, so there's the opportunity to influence the design of the product and its feature set
- it's likely to be included in the Adobe Creative Cloud suite and subscription models, so if you're already using Creative Cloud, you should have Adobe XD included in your subscription

Cons:

- as it's in beta, there are features absent and problems with the ones that have been implemented; that said, it's likely that these problems will be ironed out as the app moves into production releases
- although designs are vector-based and scale across different viewports, there's no sign of features to support adaptive or responsive design
- the support for high-fidelity designs stops short of supporting the design of complex interactions (for example, presenting different states based on user input); however, this may be added to the product as it develops and matures
- tools for supporting the creation of prototypes with real content currently seems limited to imagery; there are no tools to help create placeholder text, or to import or use content from external data sources

■ assuming Adobe bundle XD into the Creative Cloud suite subscription when it comes out of beta, you'll require a Creative Cloud license to use it if you're yet to buy one

Comparable tools:
We're unaware of any one single tool that is clearly comparable to Adobe XD in terms of aims and feature set. But it's arguably comparable to using combinations of other tools, such as Sketch and InVision, or Sketch and the Craft plugin (the latter is discussed in Appendix A).

Summary

In this chapter, we've looked at a selection of tools that you can use to create designs, and interactive prototypes from those designs.

Many of these tools would typically be regarded as sitting in the domain of UI and UX designers (or workers who perform UX/UI design as a part of their jobs); these designers have used tools such as Balsamiq and Axure to design wireframes and layouts for some years now. Now that prototyping is increasingly becoming part of the workflow of design and product teams, the feature set of these tools has broadened to help support teams who create and share interactive prototypes. In contrast to these tools, we've also looked at the popular option of using Keynote and PowerPoint for prototyping. Since these tools are ubiquitous and well understood by many who are *not* UX experts or designers, they're certainly worth consideration for prototyping.

Throughout the chapter, we've looked at tools that cover different ranges on the prototype visual fidelity spectrum. Balsamiq is well-suited to the creation of quick sketch-style, low-fidelity prototypes, while Adobe XD can be used to create production-level fidelity prototypes. And OmniGraffle and Axure sit somewhere in the middle, creating good-quality wireframe-style prototypes. Keynote and Prototype operate across this spectrum.

Looking beyond visual fidelity, the level of support for interaction design these tools offer varies as well. Axure stands out as a tool containing a powerful set of features to support all kinds of interactions. With this impressive feature set comes a steep learning curve—and a hefty price tag. Additionally, the tools we've covered offer varying degrees of support for the use of real (or at least realistic) content and data, which help to make prototypes more realistic and hence engaging.

In the next chapter, we're going to look at the prototyping tool set that arguably offers the most flexibility in terms of the kind of prototypes created: HTML prototypes.

Chapter

7

Building HTML Prototypes

When we say **HTML prototypes**, we mean a website comprising HTML markup, CSS for presentation, and JavaScript for additional interactivity. It may be a simple HTML website, or a website that runs on a framework or content management system (CMS).

This chapter is *not* a detailed step-by-step guide; nor will it teach you how to use HTML, CSS, JavaScript, or frameworks. It aims to help you understand all the options for creating HTML prototypes and their benefits. You'll find out what's needed to get started, and gain some guidance on how to approach creating an HTML prototype. We'll also include some real-life prototyping case studies from some of the projects we've worked on at fffunction.

After reading this chapter, you should be able to make an informed decision as to what approach will suit you and your project.

The Pros of Using HTML

Let's look at the benefits of employing HTML prototypes.

Responsive Design

Significantly, the only way of creating a truly responsive prototype that works across multiple devices and screen sizes is with an HTML prototype.

Flexibility

An HTML prototype can be as close to—or far from—the real thing as you want it to be. Prototypes can be ready to move into production with few amendments if you so desire, or they can be kept quick and dirty for a lower fidelity experience if that suits your needs.

Complex Interactions

With HTML prototypes, you're able to produce complex interactions involving web technologies; for example, saving data a user enters into a prototype and revealing it later on, or altering the content user sees based on their selections.

Latest Technology

The building blocks of the Internet are constantly evolving at a fast rate. You can take advantage of this and bring the latest tools and techniques into your prototype.

Resources

Many resources exist to help you in the form of tutorials, tools, and frameworks.

Source Control for Collaboration

Using Git version control when collaborating on a prototype makes it amazingly resilient. Multiple people can work on it at the same time and commit changes without worrying about files being overwritten.

Source Control for a Historical Record

Source control also means you have a permanent historical record of all states of the prototype codebase. This is especially useful if you need to demonstrate what you have done in the past—often a requirement of public sector or grant funded projects.

Various Sources of Content

Content can be integrated into the prototype in different ways. Content creators can join in the process either directly in the prototype, or in another space they are more familiar with, such as a text file or CMS.

Accessibility

If you're going to employ a prototype with an audience that has accessibility requirements, HTML prototyping is the way to go. You can test your prototype with tools and services as you build to ensure your creation is accessible. It also enables you to test with users in their standard situation and setup.

Speed of Change

Once set up, it can be super quick to show the effect of simple design in an HTML prototype, especially content changes. You can often mockup quick ideas during a review session and show it live in the browser straight away, or use browser tools to "live edit" the page on the fly. Other tools often require a publishing or export stage before you can show changes made.

And a Few Cons of HTML

While there aren't too many, be alert to a few issues you may encounter when utilizing HTML prototypes.

Learning Challenges

HTML prototyping is harder to pick up than the other techniques we've covered. It's technical, and there's more than one thing you need to learn. A lot of resources and support exist to help you, and if you have the time to learn, it could save you time later on. Seek out the help of a developer with the more technical aspects and use your time to make quick progress on designing the prototype.

Experience Limitations

As has been mentioned, there's a lot to learn if you're new to HTML and CSS. Your prototype's design and interaction concepts might be too challenging to make yourself, or its functionality limited by what you can create. This is completely experience-dependent, so you should seek to partner with a developer if you can. Bear in mind the other techniques we've outlined in this book, and switch the tool you use to allow you to prototype as quickly and easily as possible. Prototyping a complex micro interaction in HTML, CSS, and JavaScript could be a lot easier using Keynote or PowerPoint, for example.

Planning is a Must

Avoid diving straight into code; instead, plan what you are going to prototype first—covered next in this chapter. It's likely an HTML prototype comes further along in the design process, after you have defined your product. It's possible you have built other lower fidelity prototypes already.

Your HTML Prototype Planning Kit

When you begin building your HTML prototype, there are few basics you should have in place.

User Research

Design with the user in mind, so take the time to collect and digest any available research outcomes or user personas. Knowing your users up front will help you avoid creating an experience that will fail for certain audiences that you only find out about when you come to test with them.

Content

If content is available, or you're able to create it, then utilize this; it will be a massive help having this information up front. There might be a content strategy in place or style guide to help you. It can be done in a team: while one person is building a prototype, another is writing content. It may not be production-ready content, but you should have an understanding of what content is on a page. Using draft content is better than dummy text and placeholder images.

Structure and Functionality

Know which templates and pages need creating, and the purpose of each one. A variety of sources such as user journeys, information architectures, sitemaps, or a functional specification can help inform your structure. If you're unsure, crack open some sticky notes and start a structure yourself—it should be quick to take shape. Make notes on what happens on each page; we recommend each page containing just one purpose or action so you can then rearrange them to find the right flow.

Skills Required

How you approach building HTML prototypes depends on your skill set. If you have experience of front-end development or a working knowledge of using

HTML and CSS, it's possible to develop the prototype from scratch yourself. Even with a little knowledge you can use available frameworks, such as Bootstrap or Foundation, or CMS themes to give you a head start creating the necessary designs.

If you lack front-end development skills but know a developer with them, you can work as a team. Collaborating with a person who knows their way around HTML, CSS, and JavaScript will enable building really high-fidelity prototypes. Later, we'll cover how two people can work on the same prototype at the same time by using Git for source control. A developer can also help with setting up a CMS, also covered later in this chapter.

When collaborating with a developer, it's always worth having them involved earlier rather than later. Showing previous prototypes, user-testing sessions, and other related research will help having a shared understanding of the project sooner. The developer can also contribute to the design of the prototype as you decide what to build together.

Collaborative working need not just be with a developer. Writers and other members of your team can be involved and add real content to your prototype, while designers can help with the visual appearance. By taking a team approach and assigning different people tasks, you can really ramp up the speed at which a prototype takes shape.

Tools for Rapid Prototyping

Prototyping should be fast, so lets look at some tools that will help you create prototypes quickly.

Preprocessors for Writing CSS

CSS preprocessors can save a lot of time and effort by enabling you to write CSS faster. While that can be done straight into a CSS file, it's better to use a language such as Sass[1] or Less[2]. We'll now look at Sass because that's what we use at fffunction, but similar features are available in other preprocessors, such as Less.

There are several reasons to use CSS preprocessors for prototyping. One is the use of *variables*. Setting a variable name and value enables you to then reference it in the rest of your code. For example, a color: `$primary-color: #FF5733`; It's easier to remember the variable name than a hex code, and if it needs changing, you only have to do so in one place.

Another reason is the ability to *nest selectors*. This allows you to structure your Sass in the same way as you structure your HTML, which is useful if you're still learning the ropes or collaborating. Nesting can result in large file sizes of the compiled CSS file, leading to slower page load times. Yet generally you won't be too concerned with how fast a site loads with prototypes, so nest as much as you like. Speed of coding is a priority, after all.

You can also create *partial Sass files* for inclusion in other Sass files. For example, `_colors.scss` could be a file for all your color variables, which can then be imported into other Sass files using the `@import` command. This keeps your code organized and makes it simpler for you and your collaborators to find values needing to be changed.

Finally, you can make *mixin* functions, which can help save a good deal of time not having to write repetitive chunks of code. Even better—lots of mixins are already available for you to copy into your codebase and start using. No need to even know how to create them. The following example is a mixin that defines a link style you can apply to any element:

```
// Defining the mixin function
@mixin linkstyle ($linkcolor) {
    color: $linkcolor;
    text-decoration: none;
    &:visited {
        color: darken($linkcolor, 10%);
    }
    &:hover {
```

---

1. http://sass-lang.com
2. http://lesscss.org

```
        border-bottom: 1px solid darken($linkcolor, 10%);
        color: darken($linkcolor, 10%);
    }
    &:active {
        border-bottom: 1px solid darken($linkcolor, 10%);
        color: darken($linkcolor, 10%);
        position: relative;
        top: 1px;
    }
}

// Apply it to an element
.typeset a {
    @include linkstyle(#F25111);
}
```

There's a good introductory article on SitePoint to using mixins[3] and a great library of mixins called Bourbon[4] that's free for you to use.

Turning the Sass code you write into CSS requires a preprocessor, which can be done using an application or command line interface (CLI) terminal method. Additionally, here are some tools that will watch your Sass or Less files for changes and automatically compile them into CSS:

- CodeKit: https://codekitapp.com
- Compass: http://compass-style.org
- Koala: http://koala-app.com
- Prepros: https://prepros.io

For a guide on how to get started with Sass, check out *Jump Start Sass*[5] from SitePoint.

[3.] https://www.sitepoint.com/sass-basics-the-mixin-directive/

[4.] http://bourbon.io

[5.] https://www.sitepoint.com/premium/books/jump-start-sass/

Tools for Interactivity

In some prototypes, you may need to add interactivity on top of the native functionality provided by HTML; for example, a tab design or date picker. JavaScript can be used to add such interactivity. Whether you're a developer with knowledge of JavaScript or not, we'd recommend using the JavaScript library jQuery[6] to help speed up the process of creating additional or custom functionality.

jQuery provides a set of functions that are like shortcuts to what would otherwise be more complex JavaScript functions. They're intuitively named—you can probably guess as to what the following common functions do:

- `.addClass`
- `.fadeIn`
- `.remove`
- `.slideDown`

The simplest use of jQuery is to alter the class of an HTML element and allow CSS to define the appearance. There are a lot of possibilities just using this approach alone.

On top of jQuery, you can add the jQuery user interface library[7]. This goes a step further, providing a library of interface elements that you can readily use in a prototype such as:

- accordions
- datepickers
- dialog boxes (modal)
- menus
- progress bars
- sliders
- tabs
- tooltips

---

6. https://jquery.com
7. https://jqueryui.com

Other sources of ready-made elements you can include are CoDrops [8] and Bootsnipp[9]. There are many others online, and you can also borrow elements from frameworks such as Bootstrap and Foundation, which we'll cover soon.

It's also worth considering how you can add forms to your site. Forms generally rely on server-side code such as PHP to process the fields and send the information elsewhere, and this can be tricky to get working properly. If the capture of information from forms is a requirement, try using a service such as Formspree[10], which forwards form information to your email address and is simple to set up. For more advanced options, take a look at FormBucket[11], FormKeep[12], or Formlets[13].

In some cases, you might have a more complex requirement of taking submitted form data or recording actions completed by a user, then using this data to decide what you show next, keeping it as part of the user's session. This is getting into fairly technical territory, so you may need to enlist the help of a developer. You might be prototyping the creation of an account, and wanting to populate the prototype with the data submitted as part of the registration process. To do this, you can set cookies on a user's browser, or use local storage capabilities to store form data. You can then pull out that data later in the user's journey and use it to adapt the prototype's content. This avoids awkward moments in a user-testing session, such as "Let's pretend you picked this option." We'll look at a real-world example of one of our projects at fffunction at the end of the chapter.

There are frameworks that provide this functionality, such as the GDS Prototype Kit, which we'll talk about shortly. Speaking of which, we should move onto how using a framework can help.

[8.] https://tympanus.net/codrops/

[9.] http://bootsnipp.com

[10.] https://formspree.io

[11.] https://www.formbucket.com

[12.] https://formkeep.com

[13.] https://www.formlets.com

Making Headway with Frameworks

Speed is one of the key elements of prototyping and getting a head start using prebuilt elements, or frameworks, is a great way to save time. Frameworks are collections of functional modules and templates that can be used to build a website. They vary from being quite basic—just enough to get you going with a creating a responsive website with native HTML elements—to fully featured with complicated design elements such as accordions, tabs, and off-canvas navigation.

Picking the right framework is a case of considering the feature set best able to deliver the head start you need. Consider also the coding skills you have, your familiarity with different templating languages, and the methods of running prototypes.

Essentially, the goal is to pick the one that will allow you to do the most amount of building in a short space of time.

Let's now look at the more popular frameworks.

Bootstrap

Bootstrap[14] is really popular and has many features. It originated from the design team at Twitter to encourage consistency and reduce maintenance across internal tools. Since then it's been made open source and grown over the years to keep up with developments in the industry. At the time of writing, version 4 is being prepared for release, further improving the framework and moving the grid system to use Flexbox.

Bootstrap contains a comprehensive array of basic elements:

- responsive grid
- typography
- tables, including responsive tables
- forms
- buttons
- images

[14.] http://getbootstrap.com

helpers, including some that help with accessibility

Additionally, these common design patterns are also included:

- accordions
- alerts
- carousels
- dropdown menus
- icons (removed in version 4)
- pagination
- panels and cards
- tabs

When you start working with it, you'll find it's very well documented with several example page layouts included to help you along. There is also a "Customize and download" page, which enables you to select parts of the frameworks code for inclusion. Furthermore, it enables control of a great number of variables to configure the framework. You can adjust colors, sizes, number of columns, and other values to give you a personalized version of Bootstrap.

Everything you need is there to get up and running quickly, assembling HTML into a prototype without having to alter the CSS or JavaScript. If you want to edit the CSS, version 3 uses Less with a Sass version available; at the time of writing, version 4 will use Sass alone.

If you'd like help starting with Bootstrap, *Jump Start Bootstrap*[15] published by SitePoint can help.

Foundation

Foundation[16] is much like Bootstrap, both being the two most popular frameworks on the Web. Googling "Bootstrap vs Foundation" will provide a view of an almost endless debate as to which is better. The truth is it's almost always going to be a personal preference. Once you start using one, you're likely to stick with it as the time invested in learning grows.

[15.] https://www.sitepoint.com/premium/books/jump-start-bootstrap
[16.] http://foundation.zurb.com

Foundation has a few useful features that Bootstrap lacks; for instance, a form validation script called Abide. There is an add-on called Joyride that enables you to easily set up a "tour" of your prototype to onboard new users. There's also a more advanced off-canvas navigation pattern to use, and more example templates.

One feature highlights a key difference in the two: Bootstrap is more intended to be used as is, while Foundation is more geared towards being built upon. Panini is Foundation's templating engine and flat file compiler. It enables using templates to build out a prototype with included partials, variables, and helpers. This allows rapid development of custom prototypes using Foundation.

Help starting with Foundation is also covered by SitePoint: see *Jump Start Foundation*[17].

Pattern Lab

Pattern Lab[18] is both powerful and complex. Initially, it has a steep learning curve if you're unfamiliar with the technologies used, but some of the features make this worthwhile.

With Pattern Lab, you have both a framework to use and a pattern library in which to use it. That's potentially quite useful if you need to document elements of your prototype as you go. It also gives you controls to navigate from pages to the components that make up the framework, known as atoms, molecules, organisms, and templates, as illustrated in figure 7-1. If you're already familiar with the principles of atomic design[19], this system will be familiar to you.

---

[17]. https://www.sitepoint.com/premium/books/jump-start-foundation
[18]. http://patternlab.io
[19]. http://bradfrost.com/blog/post/atomic-web-design

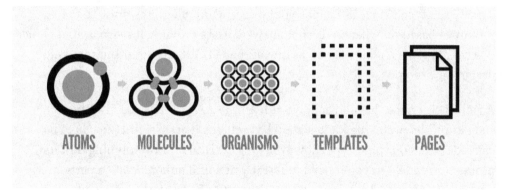

7-1. The components of atomic design

Controls are also available to determine the viewport size, which is very useful if you need to demonstrate how a design responds to different device sizes.

Pattern Lab comes in several different flavors depending on what environment you favor. There are PHP versions that use Mustache, Twig, and Drupal-ready (Twig) templating languages, and Node versions that use Gulp or Grunt. Starter kits also exist for Foundation, Bootstrap, and Material Design to give you common elements with which you may already be familiar. The most fully featured is the base demo kit, though, so it's worth starting there.

Another powerful feature of Pattern Lab is its ability to work with data. It enables you to do this using JSON files to store simple key and value pairs. We'll talk about how powerful an ability this is later in the chapter.

Skeleton

Skeleton[20] is a simple starter framework. It has a grid system and basic HTML modules with CSS, such as typography, tables, lists, forms, and so forth. It's easy to get up and running and is available with Sass and Less versions if you're using them with which to build.

GDS Prototype Kit

If you want to build a functional journey where a user is entering information into a series of forms, it's worth looking at the UK Government Digital Service's

---

20. http://getskeleton.com

(GDS) Prototype Kit[21] . It enables you to create unique routes through the prototype based on what choices or answers users provide. It's also a great choice if accessibility is a requirement, as one of the ten GDS design principles is to design for everyone.

As all GDS services have to achieve at least the AA WCAG accessibility standard[22], its prototype kit is a good base choice if accessibility needs to be catered for in your prototype; however, "it's designed for prototyping, not for production code," so you'll need to test it yourself if adherence to a particular standard is needed. It's more complex than other frameworks covered here, but is very well documented, so you should be able to have it up and running in a matter of hours.

All the Frameworks

There are many other frameworks out there, and they are well worth exploring. You should always try to fit the framework to the project, as opposed to the other way around. Here are some further frameworks worthy of your attention:

- Bulma: http://bulma.io
- Concise CSS: http://concisecss.com
- Material Design Light: https://getmdl.io
- Pure CSS: http://purecss.io
- Semantic UI: http://semantic-ui.com
- Spectre: https://picturepan2.github.io/spectre
- UI Kit: https://getuikit.com

Using Content in Prototypes

As we mentioned way back in Chapter 1, prototyping with real content will always create a better outcome for your prototype's intended purpose. This not only makes the prototype seem more realistic, but it actually could form part of what you are trying to test.

[21.] https://govuk-prototype-kit.herokuapp.com
[22.] https://www.w3.org/WAI/WCAG20/quickref/

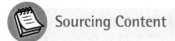

Sourcing Content

You might need to source icons and images, and we'd recommend the following:

- Nova icon set with 4000 icons: http://www.webalys.com/nova/
- Free images from Unsplash: https://unsplash.com/
- Placeholder image generator with custom text: http://placehold.it

The simplest way to add content to an HTML prototype is to copy and paste it into HTML files that make up your prototype. You'll need to know the basics of HTML text formatting to do this, but it's one of the simplest parts of HTML to pick up.

There are ways of importing content from other sources that can help, such as using JSON files to document arrays of information. **JSON** is a simple file format that stores keys and values. The Pattern Lab framework mentioned earlier in this chapter has support for reading data out of JSON files.

Here's an example of a JSON file that contains an array of data for a menu. Each of the navigation items uses the `label` value for the text of that item and the `url` value for the link. It's now easy to edit that menu by altering the values in that JSON file:

```
// JSON menu
"primaryNav" : [
    {
        "label": "About",
        "url": "about.html"
    },
    {
        "label": "Team",
        "url": "team.html"
    },
    {
        "label": "Blog",
        "url": "blog.html"
    }
]
```

This data is then used within templates using templating languages, such as Mustache[23]. In this example you can see the `label` and `url` values are used to create a menu item:

```
{{# primaryNav }}
 <li class="nav__item"><a href="{{ url }}">{{
↪ label }}</a></li>
{{/ primaryNav }}
```

There are other templating languages that are capable of working in this way and you can also us JavaScript to pull out content from a JSON file into an HTML page.

It's also possible for people to populate these JSON files with content for use within a prototype. Copywriters can then be brought into the prototyping process, as the files are relatively easy to understand and edit.

You can find out more about JSON on SitePoint[24]

Another way of using an external source that's even better for involving copywriters and content creators is Google Sheets. Content is added to a spreadsheet, then parsed from that sheet to JSON to be used in your prototype. This gives you the ability to have multiple content editors working together in an environment with which they are familiar.

The final way we wanted to mention is exporting data from an existing website into a prototype. For example, prototyping a course finder for an education organization. There may be an existing website from which you can obtain an export of content. This could be exported as a CSV (comma-separated values) file, which could then be imported into a Google Spreadsheet. Another more common file type for exporting is XML (eXtensible Markup Language). XML can be used as a data source for prototyping as is, or easily converted to JSON. That data can then be read into an HTML page using JavaScript.

[23.] https://mustache.github.io
[24.] https://www.sitepoint.com/basics-json-syntax-tips/

Using a Content Management System (CMS)

So far in this chapter, we've dealt with creating a prototype from scratch, or by using a framework. Another way is to use a content management system, or CMS. This offers you several benefits, the clue being in the name: content management.

It helps in using real content by providing an admin interface to manage that content. This interface enables you to bring content editors and other team members into the process. Collaboration becomes easy, and several people can work simultaneously to populate your prototype with content.

Setting up a CMS, however, is rarely an easy experience for beginners. It's better to seek the support of a developer, and then concentrate on the actual design of the prototype once it is set up.

Content management systems all come with an array of common features that will help you implement complex features into your prototype quickly and easily. It also makes it easy to edit, too. These features include:

- uploading, processing, and adding metadata to media
- adding, configuring, and updating menus
- showing lists or groups of content dynamically
- adding taxonomies to group together content, or form dynamic relationships between different types of content
- pagination

You may also be able to take your code forward into the development of a product, or perhaps the content of your prototype can be migrated or exported to save you repeating the effort of collating, organizing, and uploading. We'll talk more about this later in the chapter.

In many content management systems there is the concept of a **theme**: a group of templates that have a specific design and functionality. In most cases there are simple base themes that developers can utilize when starting a project. An example is the Underscores Wordpress theme[25] developed by Automattic (the organization behind Wordpress). This functional theme has very little styling; it's

---

[25.] http://underscores.me/

intentionally a blank canvas to start with, but the website has a nice option of being able to customize the theme name and whether it uses Sass or not before downloading. Many of these base themes are good places to start.

For our purposes here, in most cases you'd want to avoid muddying the waters by presenting a prototype that's too polished. This will render most of the themes out there unusable without you having to rip out the style while keeping the layout of a theme. Selecting a simple *vanilla* theme is the best way to go. In many cases your prototype is being built to test functionality, labeling, or usability, so it's best to make them very simple monochromatic experiences. You could possibly use color for calls to action or alert messages, but you'll want to avoid the possibility of a prototype's visual appearance causing issues with what you are testing.

If you go through this process more than once, you'll find that you start to build up a theme of your own to use for prototyping. At fffunction, we have base themes in place that we use to start the build of all our projects, and they can be also used for prototypes.

In addition, content management systems usually have a collection of plugins around them to extend the functionality of the core application. Again, these enable you to quickly add functionality and features that would otherwise take days to create.

Example CMSs Used for Prototyping

There are many CMSs available, so to be non-partisan about making recommendations we'll only speak from experience here. Here are some of the content management systems we've used in our work over the years at fffunction.

Wordpress

Wordpress[26] is well supported with a straightforward installation process—ideal if you've yet to use a CMS. There is also a massive community behind it, so it's very easy to find help if you get stuck.

[26.] https://wordpress.org

Perch

Perch[27] is a lightweight CMS built on PHP. You can add it to an existing HTML website or prototype to make it content-manageable, or start from scratch to build a prototype. As Perch is a paid product, there is support from the developers should you need it.

Statamic

Statamic[28] is a **flat file** CMS. This means that the site reads its content from a collection of files, rather than rely on a database of any kind. These files are commonly written in TXT or Markdown format, which is incredibly easy to pick up. Flat file CMSs are a growing breed; another we've used is Kirby[29].

Creating Accessible Prototypes

You may have accessibility as a priority for your prototypes; if that's the case, using an HTML prototype is really the only way to do this successfully. When it comes to preparing an accessible prototype, WaveAIM[30] tools are useful for checking accessibility. You can also run the prototype through screen readers to check how it will present your content. This can be done yourself by using the native Mac screen reader, or NVDA on a Windows machine. We'd recommend going for NVDA if possible as it has a wide user base.

The already mentioned GDS kit isn't tested for accessibility, but we think it would make a good base with which to start, particularly if it's used in conjunction with the UK Government's Frontend Toolkit[31].

[27.] https://grabaperch.com
[28.] https://statamic.com
[29.] https://getkirby.com
[30.] http://wave.webaim.org/
[31.] https://github.com/alphagov/govuk_frontend_toolkit

Making Prototypes Available Online

Once you've built your prototype, you need to put it somewhere to show others. You will have built your prototype utilizing your computer, using a local development environment to work in. While your prototype can be run on your own machine, you'll need to move it online for others to see it. Depending on the tools you've used, you can do this in a variety of ways.

Sharing Your Prototype Remotely

Sometimes you'll want to show a prototype on your local machine to a person not with you. You might want to use the prototype to explain a point, or a team of people could be working collaboratively in different places and need to discuss an issue. A product we've used to enable this is Finch[32]. Finch creates a URL that lets people access the prototype on your local machine, yet keeps the rest of your computer secure. It only works while your machine is online, however, so you'll need another option if the people you're sharing it with need to see it at a later date.

Moving Flat File Prototypes Online

If you have a static HTML prototype, or one that has been exported to static HTML, you need a way of moving those files to a server to show them online. At fffunction, we use Surge[33]. It's super simple and either generates a domain for your prototype, or you can use a custom domain you already own.

Moving Content-managed Prototypes Online

If you're using a content-managed prototype, or if you've used a framework that relies on back-end code running, putting that prototype online is a little more complex. Whichever CMS or framework you've used should come with documentation on how to host it. You'll probably first need to set up a server and

---

[32.] https://meetfinch.com

[33.] https://surge.sh

domain name to show files. Once that's done, transfer the files there using FTP software such as FileZilla[34], or use deployment services.

Tools to Automate Deployment

Rather than manually moving files when working on a prototype, there are ways to automate deployment so that your online prototype is kept up to date. If you have gone down the route of using source control with a Git repository, use online services to manage the migration—or deployment—of code to a server. You can go further and automate that deployment every time you make a commit to a branch, too, so your online prototype stays up to date. At fffunction we use DeployHQ[35] and DeployBot[36] for this task.

Managing Databases

You may need to migrate databases from your local machine to a live site if you're using one, or vice versa if you want to take a database from a live site and use it on your local machine. Hosting accounts usually come with a tool to help you manage databases. It's worth making database backups before migrating to save you from mistakes. Backups also make a useful history in case you want to move back to a previous version of the prototype. Again we're in technical territory here, so finding a developer to help would be wise.

Hosting Providers

If you require a hosting account to run your prototype, we'd recommend looking at Digital Ocean[37]. It's a platform that enables you to run multiple servers, and costs about $10 a month. You might need to add Server Pilot[38] for a LAMP setup to run PHP content management systems such as Wordpress, Laravel, or Drupal.

[34.] https://filezilla-project.org
[35.] https://www.deployhq.com
[36.] https://deploybot.com
[37.] https://www.digitalocean.com
[38.] https://serverpilot.io

Another option is Heroku[39], which is free and can be configured to update automatically when you commit code to your Git repository. This could be a quicker way to get things set up, as no cost is involved and no IT department is needed.

Throwaway versus Reusable Code in HTML Prototypes

Prototypes should be quick and dirty; however, there are possibilities here to reuse elements of a prototype in the final version of a product.

Developers rarely write code for the same functionality from scratch every time; they create snippets that can be reused or, better still, independent modules of code that can be dropped into projects repeatedly and hooked up. There is always the temptation to keep parts of an HTML prototype's codebase, and if you bear this in mind when building it, you can identify what parts you will want to take forward into production. You can then create these parts with a little more rigor than you might otherwise do.

Be aware, though, of the dangers involved in moving prototype code into production.

Using Sass can be super quick if you abandon considerations of the final CSS file's code size; however, if you fail to address this and refactor it, you could be introducing performance issues in your website just in terms of download time.

In most of the final use cases of prototypes, such as demoing or user testing, you have control over the browser and devices it is viewed on. As a result, it's unlikely to have undergone rigorous browser and device testing.

The code may not have been created with that in mind; shortcuts, quite rightly, may have been taken and so you need to be aware of this. For example you may not have followed the principles of progressive enhancement[40], so if a technology such as JavaScript is unavailable, the user experience is broken. Similarly, you may not have designed or coded with accessibility in mind.

[39.] https://www.heroku.com
[40.] https://alistapart.com/article/understandingprogressiveenhancement

As always, you need to find the right balance, depending on what the purpose of the prototype is and who is going to be using it.

Code might be just one item you want to take forward into production; you might wish to be able to export or migrate your content as well. If you've a content creator working on the process, or a lot of data in a database or other data source, you may be able to save time by migrating it to a production-ready version. Many of the major CMSs have features that allow export and import from others.

HTML Prototyping Case Studies

In this final part of the chapter, we look at some of the HTML prototypes we've built at fffunction and explain the process of each.

Dorothy House Hospice Care

The Problem

When Dorothy House[41] came to us with a brief, the main issue with their existing site was that users found it hard to navigate to the information they needed. The site had a lot of organic content growth over time, and three main user groups who each required a unique tone of voice in terms of content.

[41.] https://www.dorothyhouse.org.uk/

Volunteer in a shop

More than 700 people volunteer for us in our 28 shops and resorting centre. Their efforts make a huge difference – our shops provide us with over 10% of our income. There are plenty of different roles available, in a range of locations. So why not consider joining our team? It's a great chance to gain new skills and meet new people.

Here are just a few ways you could get involved:

Sorting volunteer – Help to sort, prepare, research, price and present goods donated for sale.

Driver – Transfer the stock between shops and pick up donations of large furniture.

Steaming volunteer – Use the steaming process to help prepare donated clothes and fabric items for sale on the shop floor.

Tills and customer service – Serve and help customers in our shops. Receive donations, take payments for goods, enter transactions into our tills, and sign people up for Gift Aid.

To find out about vacancies in your area, please get in touch with your local shop

7-2. Dorothy House Hospice Care

The Solution

Based on existing research the Dorothy House team had done, as well as our own user research, we created a new information architecture. This was the main element we needed to prototype and test with users to ensure they could find the right information. We built out a Wordpress website using a basic prototype theme we'd developed. As you can see from the screenshot, the design was kept really simple and almost unstyled; it didn't need to be beautiful to test whether users could navigate it. We used a mix of dummy and real content where it was available. There were no really interactive elements on the site; we just wanted to confirm users could find what they were looking for.

We developed scenarios from the key tasks we'd worked out in user research and ran moderated tests with users. Examples of the scenarios we asked them to test were:

You'd like directions to our Trowbridge Outreach Centre. Where would you find that information?

- You want to work at your local Dorothy House shop. How would you find out if there's a vacancy?
- You'd like to enter the Bath Midnight Walk. Where would you go for that?

For the most part users could find the information they needed. There was one exception, though. We tested medical professionals, carers, and people who wanted to help Dorothy House. Each of those users had a scenario that essentially asked them to look for job advertisements on the website. They each looked in different places: the medical professionals under *Professionals*; the carers under *About*, and the "helpers" under *Shops*. This signposted an important consideration as we went forward in the design process: people look in different places for jobs. While they might all look to be organized in one place from a content/structure perspective, jobs needed to be available in multiple places within the website.

The Outcome

We came out of this process with a tried and tested—and refined—information architecture that we were confident solved the old website's issues. As we had built the prototype in Wordpress, we were able to take the structure forward into production and use the content we'd already inserted in the CMS as a base for the live website.

You can read more about the project in a case study on our site[42] .

An Online Store

The Problem

cxpartners[43] wanted to demonstrate a new way of how an online supermarket website could work, so they commissioned us to build a prototype to do this. The prototype focused on how products could be grouped and filtered, and how we could create a better experience for users as they shopped online, and can be seen below.

[42.] https://fffunction.co/does/dorothy-house-hospice-care/
[43.] https://www.cxpartners.co.uk/

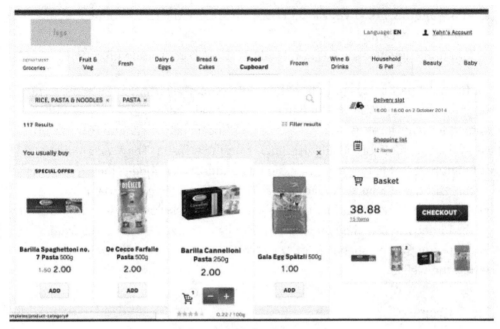

7-3. Supermarket online shop prototype

The Solution

To create this prototype we needed products, and lots of them. We lacked the time to set up a database and associated code, so instead we created a data store in a JSON file. A member of the cx team could then think about the collation and organization of products while we focused on building the prototype templates. It enabled us to rapidly prototype the filtering of products using the data store and spend some time designing some nice interactions centered around the online shopping experience.

The Outcome

The prototype was part of cxpartners' pitch to work with this client, and they won. The client loved the new thinking and approach, and commissioned them.

MacGuffin

The Problem

MacGuffin is an innovative short story platform that presents stories in audio and text format. It allows authors to publish short stories in both formats. These stories are able to be tagged by users to create a **folksonomy**, or collection of social tags, which forms a way of navigating them. There's also an analytical element that captures user behavior on the site, so data can be collected about how they consume the content.

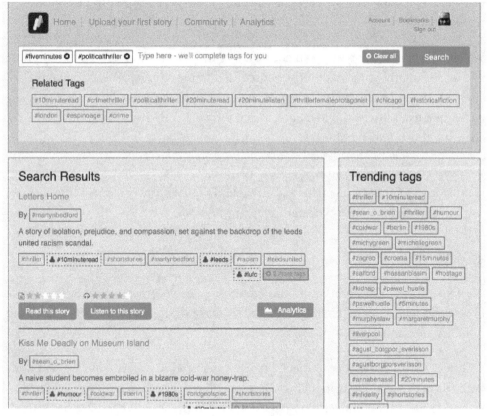

7-4. MacGuffin prototype

The problem? This is all fairly innovative so we had to make sure that what we designed would work with the audience. This meant building and testing a prototype with users.

The Solution

We built an HTML prototype as part of the design process and used it for several tasks, rather than having one clear goal.

The prototype enabled us to experiment with the design of the product and make decisions. For example, we prototyped the experience of reading and moving between written and spoken word. By calculating the position of the story against its length in text view, we were able to roughly work out where to start the HTML audio player when a user changed formats while consuming a story, giving them an almost seamless transition. We created a control bar for the prototype, so we were able to switch different aspects around and experiment with the way it worked and looked.

We faked a user signing up to an account and uploading their first story. We did this by storing the information they submitted in browser cookies so it would appear that the prototype had a functional back end, or CMS. This was then tested in a usability testing lab and refined to make sure users found the onboarding process really simple.

We were also able to get an editor from the project team involved in adding some short stories to a JSON file. This meant we didn't need to work on adding the content and could focus on designing the prototype.

The Outcomes

We were able to use prototyping throughout the design process, which enabled us to work collaboratively in a team, helped us make design decisions, validated our thinking, and constantly improved the product.

As it was a Nesta[44]-funded project, we were required to report what we had done with the prototype. We were using Git for version control, so we were able to go back in time to show the various stages of the prototype as it evolved, pointing out what testing told us and how that shaped the product.

You can read more about the MacGuffin project on our website[45].

---

44. http://www.nesta.org.uk/
45. https://fffunction.co/does/macguffin/

BBC Nature Prototype iPad App

The Problem

Together with James Chudley of cxpartners, we worked with the BBC Earth team to develop a prototype of an iPad app. The app's purpose was to create an immersive experience that blended some interactive media from the BBC Survival series with a storytelling experience. Having sketched out and created a prototype, we had a choice to make about how a user would interact with the story elements as shown below: should the app scroll vertically or horizontally. We wanted to ensure it was intuitive to users.

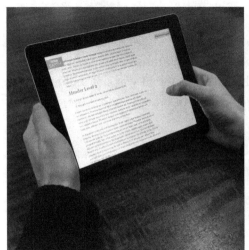 

7-5. BBC Earth prototype

The Solution

We prototyped an HTML version of the app and set it to run in full-screen mode, so that it looked like a native iPad app to the user. First, we created a vertically scrolling experience with some of the text content and placeholders for media. We were using Git for version control, so we made a **branch**, or copy, of this design and altered it to scroll horizontally. What we were aiming to do was create two experiences of the same app with the same codebase.

The Outcomes

We shared this prototype over the Wi-Fi network at a stakeholder meeting so they could all view it on their own laptops and tablets. We first served up the vertical-scrolling prototype and then the horizontal version, so everyone on the team could use the prototype, interact with it, and form an idea of the experience offered by each version. A consensus was reached to move forward with the vertical approach. The cost of producing two versions of the native iOS iPad app to do this would have taken weeks of time. We achieved this in a matter of hours and days.

Summary

In this chapter, we looked at HTML prototyping and the types of projects to which it's suited. We covered a wide range of tools and resources that help to create prototypes quickly and easily. We looked at different ways of including content in prototypes and how to host them online in order to show them to others.

We also covered what work you should do before you start creating an HTML prototype, and thinking about what you are creating so as to avoid issues if you move it into a finalised website.

Lastly, we gave some real-world examples of how HTML prototypes have been used in our work at fffunction.

In the next chapter, we look at how you can use prototypes in your projects, and what prototypes can be used for.

Chapter **8**

Using Prototypes in Your Project Workflow

Way back in <u>Chapter 2</u>, we looked at the various times when you might use prototyping in your project workflow.

It is hoped you now have some ideas about the toolsets you might use to build prototypes at certain stages. We'll now look in a little more detail at some techniques for using prototypes at such stages to get the most out of them.

It's outside the scope of this book to discuss project management methodologies (or to get opinionated about them—there are plenty of others covering that ground elsewhere). So you might be doing "big A" or "little a" Agile, Kanban, Scrum, Sprints, Waterfall, some kind of hybrid of all of these, or perhaps not really following a structured methodology and just "getting on with it." That's all fine with us, because what's important is that however you manage projects, you *can* incorporate prototyping into your projects—and benefit from it—without pain and huge changes to teams and budgets.

We've already discussed why we should use prototypes in more detail in <u>Chapter 1</u>), but it's worth reminding ourselves of what prototypes can give us when we bring them into a project, including:

- assisting the design team to develop, explore, and communicate design ideas among themselves
- enabling powerful stakeholder engagement because stakeholders can see and use our designs
- helping us bring users into our design process by allowing us to explore and test our designs with real users

We're now going to discuss some tips and techniques to help you achieve these aims with various prototype toolsets.

Exploring and Communicating Design Ideas with the Team

The trick to using prototypes in your design process is to keep it lightweight, so that you can use them to try out your ideas without slowing you down. If it takes a lot of time and effort up front to set up your prototype, make changes, or share it with people, the odds are it will fail to happen.

For example, if you're using sketches to explore ideas, try using a toolset that lets you turn those sketches into prototypes, such as Marvel, or the PDF options discussed in <u>Chapter 6</u>. Or you could switch to a tool such as Balsamiq, as it allows you to think quickly in a sketch-like way and add links to create an interactive prototype.

Lots of designers like sketching because it encourages rapid, collaborative working, as seen below. With most of the simple low-fidelity prototyping tools, you only require a small amount of up-front effort to set up working practices and workflow that maintains a level of collaborative working.

Take the example of a small group of designers working alongside a client team member to sketch out ideas for new features that support advanced searching on an existing site. They have some user research (including some recordings of power users struggling to find the specific search results they need), a stack of paper, sticky notes, marker pens, and coffee. They're doing 6-8-5 sketching individually to brainstorm ideas for the search form and results list. They'll then come together to share their ideas, discuss, pick the best bits, then combine them onto larger A4 sketches stuck to the wall.

8-1. Conducting a collaborative sketching workshop

 ## 6-8-5 Sketching

6-8-5 sketching is a structured technique for encouraging individuals to come up with ideas for a design. The name comes from the aim of producing six to eight sketches in five minutes.

Participants are provided with sheets of paper or card that are divided into grids of four, six, or eight squares in which they sketch their ideas quickly.

Learn more about 6-8-5 sketching (and lots of other useful collaborative workshop activities) in the book *Gamestorming* and its accompanying website[1].

Let's bring a basic prototyping toolset into this process. We'll take a device (an iPhone or iPad, or an Android phone or tablet) that has the Marvel mobile app installed (a full description of Marvel can be found in <u>Chapter 5</u>). Each time a sketch is completed, the Marvel app is used to take a photo of the sketch. Hotspots are then added to it and it is linked together with the other pages that have already been added, seen below. We'll take a participant out of the 6-8-5 sketching process to handle this role, and to keep everyone involved with the whole process, we'll share that role around to a different person each time. Now we're creating a prototype with the most basic of workflows. It's potentially free, or at least very low-cost, depending on the Marvel plan you use.

[1.] http://gamestorming.com/games-for-fresh-thinking-and-ideas/6-8-5s/

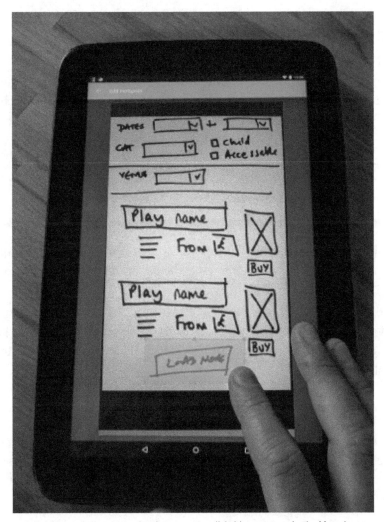

8-2. Adding a hotspot to a sketch to create a clickable prototype in the Marvel app

This prototype will be useful for the whole project team in the workshop environment. Everyone benefits from trying out the various parts of the advanced search feature in the context of a user flowing through it. It may help workshop participants to spot and raise problems with sketches that may not otherwise be apparent; for instance, in combining and stepping through the various steps combined, it becomes evident that the user journey is longer or more complicated than it need be. Or missing steps or features may be identified that hadn't been considered in the sketching process.

We could make the workshop more powerful by bringing some stakeholders or users into the process, either throughout it or at defined points (for example, after the initial morning session). As they're not experienced designers, they may struggle to visualize how sketches and ideas fit together to create an advanced search feature to use. Having the prototype available will make this much easier for them to understand, and soliciting their feedback during the workshop means that there's time to involve the whole team in resketching and adjusting the designs and prototype.

There are several options to improve this suggested basic workflow:

- use a Marvel account to sync the prototype we're creating on the device with Marvel on other devices, or a laptop/desktop with the Marvel web app open
- employ a scanner to gain better quality images of the sketches, even something like a Doxie[2] to go mobile and portable
- have workshop participants install the Marvel iOS/Android app, sign in, and add sketch photos as screens to a collaborative cloud-synced Marvel project
- give participants tablets and styluses to sketch their ideas directly into the Marvel app

 InVision Options

The workflows discussed would all work equally well with InVision (discussed in Chapter 5), except for the option of sketching directly into the app. Because InVision doesn't offer this, you'd require an additional app to complete the sketching activity, such as 53's Paper app.[3]

Engaging with Stakeholders and Project Teams

In Chapter 1, we discussed how prototypes are a great way to involve your stakeholders and get them excited in your designs. We're now going to consider some approaches to involve stakeholders using prototypes you've created.

Let's start by briefly reviewing what we mean by **stakeholders**. They're not necessarily the people who you're working directly with on a project, but they

---

2. http://www.getdoxie.com
3. https://www.fiftythree.com/

have an interest in the project's success from an organization's point of view. They might be part of an organization that will be profiled or promoted on a website. Or they could be part of a department with specific business goals that a web app you're designing is helping to meet. Typically, they're at management or senior management level (typically a Marketing Director or Vice President, Chief Marketing Officer, or Chief Technical Officer), which means they:

- are very busy
- spend a lot of time reviewing reports, spreadsheets, and slide decks
- make lots of decisions that often have an impact on money and people

As a consequence, it can be difficult to engage stakeholders with our designs, particularly in the early stages when we're coming up with ideas and trying them out, often working at low fidelity. Frustratingly, designers and project teams often find stakeholders engaging later in the process, when a design is at a higher fidelity and more developed. And, as we've discussed, making changes to our designs at that point is more expensive.

We've found that prototypes make it easier to interest stakeholders earlier, simply because a prototype can be opened and played with by stakeholders. Unlike other design deliverables—such as sitemap diagrams or wireframes—they can see how it will work without having to read explanatory notes or annotations.

When trying to engage stakeholders with your prototype, it's important that our prototypes are fast and straightforward enough to share widely. That's handy for us and our project teams: if it's hard work for us to do, we'll avoid sharing our prototypes early and often. If it's easy, we will share them. But it's also useful for the stakeholders we share with because if it's easy for them to share, they'll share with more people. They might be other stakeholders who were not directly engaged with the product, or potential user research subjects. If people are saying, "I showed it to my partner/friend/Dad and ...", it basically means you have people doing usability testing for you, for free!

We should also strive for the lowest possible barriers to people opening and stepping through our prototypes. That means avoiding them having to install apps or software; minimising platform and browser-compatibility requirements; keeping file sizes small; and making the process for opening and viewing a prototype easy enough to do without instruction or assistance.

To meet these aims, our safest bets for prototyping toolsets:

- allow us to publish our prototypes online so that they can be opened in a web browser by simply hitting a link
- create file types that can be shared via email and opened by anyone on their computers or devices

Assuming you've chosen a toolset that meets these aims to a degree—perhaps InVision/Marvel, Keynote or Powerpoint, Balsamiq generating clickable PDFs, or HTML prototypes with a suitable platform for hosting/sharing online—what's the best way to encourage stakeholders to look at your prototypes and engage with your designs? Here are our tips for making the most out of stakeholder engagement with a prototype.

Share at the Right Time, and Keep Sharing

Pick your moment wisely when sharing with stakeholders the first version of your prototype and later revisions. It's a delicate balancing act between showing a prototype that works, has a reasonable amount of content and depth, and looks coherent, versus waiting too long in order to share one that is faultless, polished, and feature-complete.

Let stakeholders know that what you're sharing with them is a work in progress, and *not* the final design. Then keep reminding them of this fact.

Encourage stakeholders to look at your prototype and give feedback often, in a way that is quick and easy for them. They shouldn't have to book time to do it. Send quick email updates as you release iterations that quickly summarize what's changed and (perhaps) why, but be aware that such notes may remain unread.

Ensure Stakeholders Are Seeing the Latest Version

If you're sharing online, try to update the prototype **in place**; that is, where the stakeholder will see it. Once you've created a link, update the prototype that the link points to. This avoids people looking at an older version of your prototype and giving you irrelevant and out-of-date feedback.

If you're sharing files, try to indicate what version it is. The most effective way is to append a date to the filename in a simple, commonly understood format. Try to nudge stakeholders into deleting earlier versions by using phrases such as "This replaces all previous versions of the prototype, which we suggest you delete."

Efficiently Use Stakeholders' Time and Attention

Avoid the need for face-to-face explanations of your prototype; stakeholders should be able to open it and get on with using it. That said, make yourself as accessible as you can to stakeholders who have queries or feedback. Be ready to open a prototype and talk it through with stakeholders when they pass your desk or bump into you in the corridor.

Aim to direct stakeholders to the part of the prototype you're most interested in them looking at at any point. Use direct links or export parts of your prototype to assist with this.

Keep Promoting the Prototype

If you have regular (weekly, monthly) status meetings that involve stakeholders, take the time to show them the latest iteration of your prototype at each meeting. Then follow up by sharing that iteration so that they're prompted to look at it.

Consider promoting your prototype everywhere you can in an unobtrusive way. Stick sketches or screenshots on the wall listing the prototype's URL to encourage everyone to view it for themselves. Add the URL at the bottom of project status reports, meeting notes, or email updates. You could even look at printing little cards or stickers to hand out to people.

8-3. Displaying the URL for a prototype on a wall display to encourage stakeholders to look at it

Be Prepared for Stakeholder Feedback

Be open and receptive to *all* feedback you receive from stakeholders. Expect to receive subjective feedback that's unhelpful, or doesn't relate specifically to your prototype; for example, colors or lack of colors, font choice ("Can you use our corporate font?"), layout, and so on. Avoid becoming defensive or dismissing this feedback, but be prepared to disregard it. The really useful feedback from stakeholders relates to their expert domain knowledge around the organization (or part of it) and its goals, so make sure you listen out for that.

Every project is different, as is every stakeholder, so observe and use your judgement as you work with them. Work out what engages each stakeholder and then adapt your workflow and strategies to make the most out of your prototypes with stakeholders.

Bringing Users into the Design Process Using Prototypes

We've talked throughout the book about how a prototype is an important way to bring users into your design process. We won't be providing a comprehensive guide to user research techniques here—that's a topic for another book. But what we can do is talk about how prototypes can make user research more efficient and effective.

The underlying benefits of having a prototype for user research are much the same as the benefits we see with stakeholders: they make it much easier for users to engage with your designs. That means that the interaction and feedback you gain from your user research participants is all the more valuable.

We'll discuss two ways (which can often overlap) you can utilize prototypes to help you learn from users:

Exploring Motivations and Behaviors in Contextual Research

When we think about users as we design, we're looking at their journey—particularly where it relates to the products and services we're designing—and considering:

- context
- motivations
- goals
- happy moments
- pain points
- measures of success

Contextual research activities help us to learn about our users, explore their journeys, and consider these aspects. Research activities are generally qualitative and can include diary studies, observation, and user interviews.

We can use prototypes to explore new angles in a contextual research activity. For example, if you're conducting user interviews, you can go armed with a selection of sketches, or a simple prototype put together with sketches or wireframes. As you discuss a participant's journey around a specific scenario, you can refer to your prototype and have your participant try it out. Or you can potentially sketch ideas out with your participant during the interview, assemble them into a prototype, and discuss them. If you're conducting a diary study, you could ask your participants to try out a specific prototype on a day when they're recording their activities.

The aim of a prototype in these scenarios is to consider how the digital product or service you're designing could fit into your participant's journey through a task. Prototypes prompt discussion and exploration around your participants' tasks and journeys. It's just as important to observe, record, and consider these discussions with your participants as it is to observe their actions with your prototype.

Testing Your Designs with Users

Observed usability tests are a great way to get high-value feedback on your designs. All that's required are:

- representative users
- a thing that presents our designs to put in front of those users

A prototype is ideal to put in front of users, irrespective of what kind of prototype it is and how it's been created.

To achieve the most out of usability tests with your prototype, keep them lightweight and do them often. Building usability tests into your project workflow and arranging participants for a round of tests in advance helps to ensure that they *will* happen. It's a good milestone to work towards with each unit of design work for your project team, regardless of what that unit may be—a sprint, a phase, a module, a feature, a week, and so on. Whatever prototype toolkits and methodologies you use, always endeavor to build in this cycle of rapid iteration and frequent usability testing.

 User Research Testing

A great book to help anyone learn how to conduct beneficial low-cost usability tests is Steve Krug's *Rocket Surgery Made Easy*[4].

Here are some basic guidelines to make the most out of usability testing with a prototype:

- Prepare simple, standalone tasks for your participants to complete using your prototype. These should evolve out of the key tasks for which you've been designing.
- Give your participants the tasks to complete one at a time, and ask them to speak their thoughts.
- If something goes wrong, or if a participant strays into an area of your prototype that's yet to be developed, step in and navigate around the problem, or abandon the task and move on.
- Focus your observations and note-taking on the problems that participants have: where they get stuck, do something unexpected, or take a wrong turn. Resist the temptation to solve issues that you see during the test session—that's a job for later.
- Think about how you can analyze as a team what you learn in usability testing, as portrayed in figure 8-4. Consider capturing the session on video, or sharing the job around your team of facilitating and observing test sessions. At the end of a round of tests, get the team together and have everyone present the key observations from each participant. Then you can work together on design ideas to solve any common problems.

---

4. https://www.goodreads.com/book/show/6658783-rocket-surgery-made-easy

8-4. Capturing and analyzing usability test observations with the project team

In-person/Remote and Moderated/Unmoderated Usability Testing

If you're new to running usability tests, we'd recommend you start simple with *moderated in-person* tests. This involves sitting down with participants in front of a laptop, desktop, or device, giving them tasks to complete with your prototype, and observing them.

Remote usability testing means using communication tools to run the tests with your participants in a remote location. Remote tests can be *moderated*, where you join the participant at an agreed time, give them tasks, and observe them via the remote communication medium. Or they can be *unmoderated*, where you use a dedicated usability testing platform to set up tasks in advance. You then share details of the test with participants for them to join and complete the test at a time that suits them, then review recordings of the test sessions later.

Remote and unmoderated usability tests can give you more flexibility in terms of recruiting participants and having them complete tests in their own time. Yet they require tools and platforms to run and capture tests, and a prototype that is shareable and complete enough to stand up to participants using it unsupervised. It's harder to deal with issues and problems that crop up in a remote test, and if the test is unmoderated, there's no way to offer help at all.

Summary

In this chapter, we've discussed specific techniques and strategies to help you build prototyping into your project workflow, and get the most out of that prototype.

We've looked at some tools and workflows to create prototypes that aid in collaborative workshop scenarios, helping to generate, share, and develop design ideas.

We've discussed how we can best use prototypes to engage stakeholders, a group who traditionally don't engage with designs as early and as often as they should.

And we've looked at some specific guidelines and techniques for bringing users into your design process by using prototypes in user research.

Which brings us to the end of the book.

What we hope we've achieved here is to have given you a solid overview of the prototyping landscape today. There are so many different tools, techniques, and approaches, and more are emerging every day (we've genuinely struggled to keep up over the six months we've been putting the book together). Whatever your level of design skill or technical proficiency, and whatever role you play in design projects, we're confident that you'll be able to pick some of these tools to try out in your design process. Your approach to prototyping and the toolsets you use will undoubtedly change and develop over time. But the key aims should remain the same: explore design ideas, engage stakeholders, and bring users into your design process.

As you continue to use prototypes in your designs, you and your teams will get more and more out of them. Your designs will be better, and your projects more effective as a result.

If you've yet to try out a tool, go and do it now—get your designs into it, and start sharing with stakeholders and users. We're confident there's no looking back!

Appendix A: Supplementary Prototyping Tools Worth Seeking

In this appendix, we highlight some other notable prototyping tools you may come across. These tools fell short of making the cut for a more detailed discussion in the chapters, possibly because they:

- are more suited to prototyping native applications (our focus has been on tools for prototyping websites and web apps)
- fail to fit easily into the structures of categories and chapters we've established
- are arguably more technical- or developer-oriented than the intended core audience for this book

There's value in briefly reviewing these tools to understand what they're about. That way you can get a feel for whether they could be useful to you and your team for creating prototypes.

Craft by InVision

Craft[1] is not a standalone prototyping tool; rather, it's a set of plugins for the Sketch design app. We briefly mentioned Sketch in Chapter 5. It's a very useful design tool for many tasks including prototype creation, and part of many designers' prototyping workflows. If you're on Mac—it's Mac-only and set to stay that way—you should definitely try it out if you've yet to already do so.

Craft is created by the clever people at InVision as part of their labs project. The various plugins add lots of useful features to Sketch to turn it into a very compelling prototyping tool in its own right. It's currently free, presumably to help encourage sales of the InVision platform. Notable features include:

- the ability to prototype effects and animations in Sketch for prototyping user interfaces
- the ability to rapidly add and update content in your prototype with Craft's data, web, and JSON integration features

[1] https://www.invisionapp.com/craft

- cloud-synced design assets to make collaborative prototype design faster and easier
- tight, simple integration with the InVision prototyping platform

8-1. Craft's image and duplicate features make it quick and easy to populate a prototype with realistic content

Facebook Origami Studio

Origami Studio[2] is a prototyping tool developed by Facebook. They've used it in the design and build processes of many of their products, including Facebook and Messenger.

It's likely to be useful primarily in designing and prototyping native apps, rather than websites and apps. We've explicitly included it here because its workflow differs greatly to all the prototyping tools we've discussed in this book.

Origami Studio is a visual tool in which prototype functionality is built by adding patches onto a canvas, then joining these patches together with connections to create a visual network, depicted below. This style of workflow is often called **Visual Programming**. If you've ever used Yahoo Pipes (a now-defunct tool that let users filter and mash up content from web feeds and web pages

---

[2.] http://origami.design/

without requiring programming skills) or made music by patching together modular synthesizers, you'll be familiar with this concept.

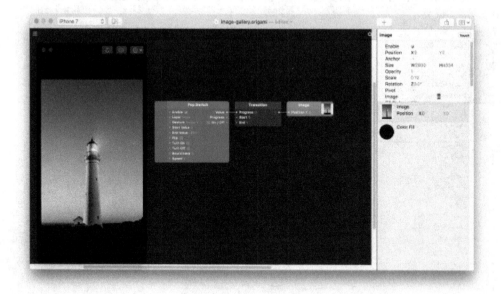

8-2. Adding patches and connections to prototype a swipe interaction on an image in Origami Studio

If you're on a Mac, reasonably technical, and designing mobile apps where you like your apps to conform to Facebook's common design language (for example, using consistent and familiar UI animations and transitions), then Origami Studio is worth a look.

Framer

Framer[3] is a tool for creating animated interactive prototypes. It's likely to be most useful for prototyping native apps but could also be used to prototype interactive websites and web apps.

Framer is worth mentioning because of its code-led workflow. Prototypes are created in Framer Studio (an Integrated Development Environment—IDE) by writing code in CoffeeScript. **CoffeeScript** is a language syntax for creating JavaScript (it's actually compiled down to JavaScript), which is intended to be simpler than writing raw JavaScript. The Framer CoffeeScript syntax is

---

3. https://framer.com/

comparable to CSS. If you've used CSS to create and style elements—and you don't run screaming from a scripting language—you should be fine using CoffeeScript to create and manipulate elements in a Framer prototype. Framer's Auto-Code feature means that you can add elements to your prototype and manipulate them through a familiar design interface, and Framer will update the CoffeeScript code on the fly for you. This can make it easier to start a project if you have limited scripting experience.

 Need more of a Coffee Fix?

Check out SitePoint's book on CoffeeScript, *Jump Start CoffeeScript*[4]. It's a great primer for helping you come to grips with it if you're using CoffeeScript in Framer, or anything else for that matter.

Framer has a significant learning curve, particularly if you've had little coding experience. That said, its Auto-Code feature makes it less intimidating than it would be otherwise to start writing CoffeeScript code. If you want to specify user interface and interaction behaviors in precise detail for your designs, it's a tool to consider.

[4.] https://www.sitepoint.com/premium/books/jump-start-coffeescript

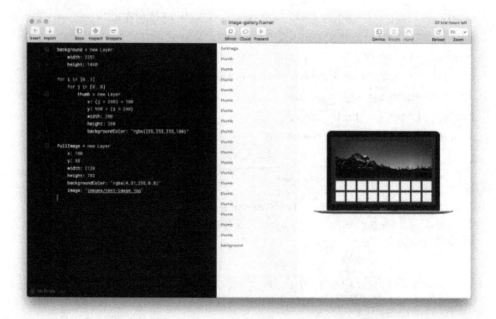

8-3. The ability to create and manipulate elements with CoffeeScript in Framer makes creating multiple thumbnails in this basic image gallery prototype fast and easy.

Principle

Much like Framer, Principle[5] is best suited to creating prototypes of native apps with its ability to prototype specific user interface interactions and animations.

It's notable because it brings in a useful design interface paradigm that some designers will be familiar with: animation timelines.

Principle prototype design assets are managed with artboards, and you can use Principle's built-in basic design tools to create and manipulate elements or import them from Sketch. The workflow should be familiar to Sketch users. Transitions between artboards are managed with connectors. It gets interesting when it comes to customizing the animations between artboards and between individual elements on specific layers in the artboards. This is managed through a timeline user interface. Its workflow will be familiar to anyone who's used tools for animation such as After Effects or Flash, or who's done some audio or video editing.

---

5. http://principleformac.com/

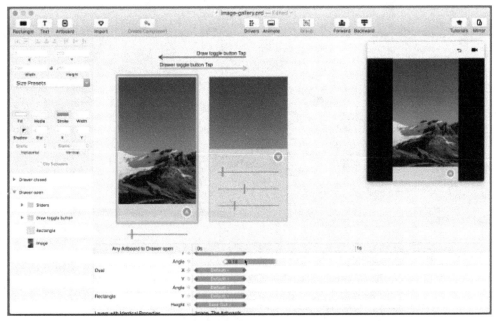

8-4. Prototyping transitions for a UI drawer opening and closing in Principle

As with Framer, if you're looking to prototype specific user interface interactions and animations with high levels of fidelity and control, Principle is a tool for consideration. It's particularly likely to suit those used to working with tools using animation timelines.

Xcode

Xcode[6] is the IDE developed by Apple for creating production-level apps for Apple products, including macOS and iOS. As such, it's a fully featured power-beast of a toolset. We're mentioning it here because it's possible to use Xcode's Interface Builder and Storyboards tools to create prototypes quickly, as shown below, and many folks do just that——particularly when they're designing and prototyping iOS or native Mac apps.

---

6. https://developer.apple.com/xcode/

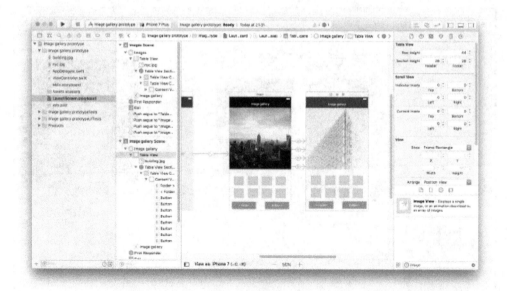

8-5. Prototyping a simple image gallery using Xcode's Interface Builder and Storyboards features

Interface Builder has a drag-and-drop interface for creating screens from elements, including buttons, toggle switches, and text fields. Storyboards allow you to set up the relationships between screens with connectors, including basic transitions such as "push" and "slide".

You can stick to built-in interface elements that give you potential consistency and fidelity of native apps. Or you can bring in your own resources, which potentially allow you to create prototypes using lower-fidelity designs such as sketches, or mockups where you can use transparent buttons overlaid on your interface elements to trigger events. If you want to go beyond basic transitions between screens, you'll have to start exploring code. With Apple's more accessible Swift programming language, this may be within your capabilities; otherwise, you'll need to work with a friendly developer.

CPSIA information can be obtained
at www.ICGtesting.com
Printed in the USA
LVHW062253300919
632799LV00004B/17/P